Hays&Hays
COMMUNICATIONS, INC.
Amarillo, Texas

PUBLISHED BY HAYS & HAYS COMMUNICATIONS, INC.
Amarillo, Texas

Dog Gone It: From Trauma to Tail-Wags, Seeing God in the Day-to-Day
Copyright © 2020 Tracy Hays

All rights reserved. No portion of this book may be reproduced, stored in a retrieval system, or transmitted in any form or by any means—electronic, mechanical, photocopy, recording, or any other—except for brief quotations in printed reviews, without the prior permission of the publisher.

Cover design by Tim Triplett

Hays, Tracy
   Dog Gone It: From Trauma to Tail-Wags, Seeing God in the Day-to-Day / by Tracy Hays
   ISBN 978-0-9789100-6-8

Printed in the United States of America.

Dog Gone It

FROM TRAUMA TO TAIL-WAGS,
SEEING GOD IN THE DAY-TO-DAY

by
Tracy Hays

To my wife, Elaine

for believing in me long before
I believed in myself.

Table of Contents

Acknowledgements iii

Introduction v

Chapter 1   The Perfect Present 1

Chapter 2   Random Compliance 9

Chapter 3   Either Way, I Get Dessert 19

Chapter 4   Exposed 27

Chapter 5   S. O. S. 35

Chapter 6   Almost, But Not Quite There 43

Chapter 7   QBKS 51

Chapter 8   Same Team 61

Chapter 9   Homecoming 69

Chapter 10   Full Circle 77

Acknowledgements

Tommy Spencer. Thanks for being a walking concordance for me. Your knowledge of scripture is extensive, yet communicated in a very practical manner. You saved me so much time pointing me toward various verses after I described what I was looking for. You grasped the heart of what I wanted to communicate and provided wise counsel. Proverbs 27:19 comes to mind when I think of you, "As water reflects a face, so a man's heart reflects the man" (NIV). I'm incredibly thankful for a friend with a true and faithful heart.

Tim Triplett. I might never have picked up the proverbial pen again if you hadn't told me you had publishing experience, both digital and print. Your expertise in this area provided the impetus to get me started. And the knowledge that you could turn my computer files into a finished product gave me the motivation to see this project through. Although your encouragement was a constant boost and greatly appreciated, it pales in comparison to the value of the reassurance you gave me on an array of topics when they were just concepts in my mind. Plus, an immense added bonus was letting you expose me to Raising Cane's for our lunches.

Lori Freeland. The signature at the bottom of your e-mails is followed by a list of the services you provide: author, editor, writing coach. While the list does a good job of describing your technical abilities, it needs to have one more word to adequately portray the complete value you bring. Confidante. I'm so thankful for the things you've taught me about writing, in addition to helping me clarify the points I'm trying to communicate through your editing. But most of all, it's been rewarding to observe my confidence grow as I learned from you. I've come to trust you and am grateful you are a safe place to pass along ideas.

Becky Davis, Taylor Hays, David Russell, Reba Russell (same last name as David, but not related), Tommy and Lana Spencer, Tim and Suzan Triplett. You guys went beyond the call of duty in being a focus group for me. While I'm appreciative of your thoughts and insights that made their way into this manuscript, they weren't nearly as valuable as your encouragement. The positive and kind words you shared were a huge dose of confidence to my uncertain mind treading in unfamiliar territory. I will be eternally grateful for the impact of your helpful and intuitive observations.

A. C. Riley and Lana Spencer. Thank you for making sure all the i's were dotted and t's were crossed. It's very comforting to have talented people come behind me to clean up my literary messes. Both of you have a firm understanding of punctuation and have made sure all the commas, periods, and quotation marks are in the right places. A. C., you have a gift for smoothing out sentences. Lana, I think I'm going to give you a new nickname – wordsmith. Thank you so much.

Introduction

My life changed in a way I could have never imagined on August 21st, 2014. After completing the majority of a forty-mile bike ride as part of my training for a half-ironman triathlon, I was struck by a car. The driver fled the scene of the accident, and a 911 call was made by a motorist who stopped to render aid. Early in 2015, I had the privilege of thanking the firefighter who arrived first at the scene. He shared that I wasn't breathing initially, and he immediately instituted the necessary procedures required to get me to breathe on my own again. Once paramedics arrived, they continued what the firefighter had begun, in addition to other life-saving measures as they loaded me in the ambulance for the drive to the hospital.

Upon arrival to the emergency room, doctors identified that I had suffered a traumatic brain injury (TBI). I was in a coma, and though no bones were broken, the prognosis was bleak. My wife, Elaine, was informed that I had less than a 20% chance of survival, and I would probably need 24/7 care for the rest of my life if I did survive.

After nearly a week had passed with no signs of improvement, my neurologist ordered a CAT scan to determine possible damage to my brain stem. He had never had a patient with significant brain stem damage recover, and his concerns were substantial. Although test results revealed that my brain stem had not been damaged, I had suffered a severe brain shear. To illustrate this type of injury, imagine shaking a bowl of Jell-O. The various cracks that would show up represent the numerous connections in a brain that have been damaged. Every TBI is unique, and only time would tell which of my brain connections were damaged or severed.

I spent four weeks in ICU, followed by four additional weeks at Baylor Rehabilitation Center in Dallas, TX, and two months at Pate Rehabilitation outside of McKinney, TX. After regaining enough strength to lift my head, relearning to stand and walk while dealing with vertigo and swallowing without aspirating into my lungs, I was released from Pate in December of 2014. My new life was about to begin. I was

Relearning to walk while pushing a cart for balance at Baylor Rehabilitation

heading home with a greatly diminished ability to read, issues with my balance and increased time required to process information, but I was heading home.

I had been in rehabilitation for almost four months and had become quite homesick. Elaine and I were beyond ecstatic that we would get to celebrate Christmas in our own home. Christmas was more meaningful to me that year as I considered how much progress I had made. My recovery was by no means complete, but I was extremely thankful that God had been so faithful to guide me this far.

Obviously, I remember nothing that took place during the initial seven days after my accident when I was in a coma. In addition, I can recall nothing about the following three weeks. It's an odd and surreal feeling to have no memories from a rather significant time of my life. But I actually count it as a blessing that I have this void. When I look at what's left of my helmet and think about the impact my head sustained, it seems more than likely that there must have been a large dose of pain when I was struck by the car, in addition to the four subsequent weeks. But if I did indeed suffer pain, I have absolutely zero remembrance of it.

But what's even harder to wrap my mind around is that other than the time mentioned above, my long-term memory is basically intact. I remember the significant events of my childhood, my high school and college years, falling in love and marrying Elaine, the birth of my four children, along with our major vacations. I am so thankful that I didn't lose these memories, as many of them represent some of the most precious experiences and occasions of my life. It would have been such a tragedy to have forgotten them.

Because of my slower pace of life, I began to think about events more deeply, make closer observations, and ponder situations more thoroughly. During my two month stay at Pate, I began to see God in the ordinary. This new speed of life was most likely a huge contributor. It's crazy to me that I can't recall anything about God showing up and protecting me during my accident. It's pretty obvious that I'm alive today due to Him showing up in a big way. But it's equally as fascinating to me to have seen God in so many small and ordinary life events.

Once I was back home and transitioned into a routine, I continued to see the Father in every-day life. This new way of seeing Him has made the simple things become profound. My hope is that as I share my experiences and insights, you also will begin to see God more frequently in the day-to-day.

CHAPTER ONE
The Perfect Present

"I've got the perfect Christmas present for you," was Elaine's confident proclamation to me a few days before Christmas. We had only been home for a couple of days but being in our own home was truly the best place to celebrate a very special holiday. We expected to be at Pate Rehabilitation for another couple of months and were thrilled for the privilege of being in our home surrounded by family. We scurried around to prepare for the arrival of our children as well as getting all of our favorite dishes prepared and of course, some last-minute shopping.

Neither of us is very good at keeping secrets, and we're possibly even worse at being surprised. So it wasn't out of character for me to begin pestering her as to her idea, and it also makes perfect sense that she caved in fairly quickly and told me that her idea was to get me a puppy.

Elaine thought a puppy might be good therapy in my emotional recovery. Before my accident, it would be safe to say I didn't fall into the "emotional juggernaut" category; however, I'd become even less emotionally communicative after my TBI. She felt a puppy would help me connect with my emotions and assist me in expressing them more freely.

The thought of adding a puppy to our lives became our main topic of conversation after Christmas had passed. We talked about whether it should be a large or medium-sized breed. Neither of us was inclined toward smaller breeds, so anything smaller than a dachshund, which was one of our previous pets, was out of the running. Then there was the shorthair versus long-hair issue, and whether to go with a breed we'd owned before or jump out there with something new. We had many great conversations, but in the end, the potential disruptions to my routines carried more weight than improving my emotional shortcomings. Elaine graciously agreed to put the puppy idea to rest.

Life rolled along for several months while trying to re-establish some structure in our lives. In the midst of medical appointments and putting our house back in order, I spent a fair amount of time getting a firm grasp on what I could and couldn't do.

Doctors at Baylor Rehabilitation had diagnosed me with alexia, and it turned out to be one of the biggest challenges facing me in my post-coma life. Alexia is different than dyslexia; it is not something you are born with; it can be acquired through a brain injury with resulting lesions. A short, but astute, description is "word blindness." It's my inability to comprehend printed words and sentences despite preservation of my ability to write. It explains why reading is such a struggle for me and the necessity of learning to read again. Although I can describe my diagnosis, I'm still coming to grips with the ramifications.

The difficulties associated with reading reared their head fairly early after returning home. I was surprised to discover that retaking my driver's license exam would be a requirement to drive again. Although the driver's license study material was a mere 45-page booklet, it required several weeks for me to complete. I struggled through studying because I desperately wanted to pass the exam. It was important to add something to my list of things I *could* do and not be totally dependent and imposing on Elaine.

Concerned about being able to finish the test within the allotted time, I spoke with the DPS office to ask about exam times and the possibility of having someone read the exam for me. It was pretty humbling to admit I struggled to read and might need extra time. Relieved to find out that there was an audial version of the test, I returned a couple of days later to take the exam and walked out of the DPS office with my head held high. I had passed! All that stood between me and the open road was completion of the driving portion of the test. And maybe my wife.

In all actuality, Elaine had been very supportive of my efforts to regain my license. Although many of our friends and family had expressed concern at my attempts to drive within a relatively short time since my accident, she understood how important it was for me to attempt things on my own and the value that would accompany my independence. After assuring me that I was more cautious and skilled than our teenagers when they began driving, I began venturing out behind the wheel. Even though I had driven very little in six months, the driving portion of the exam presented no problems. In fact, the only part I got poor marks on was parallel parking. (But doesn't everyone struggle with that?) It was so satisfying having my driver's license picture taken, and I truly relished every second of that photo op. I was elated, realizing I had passed the standards established by the State of Texas. Driving was a new activity I could do in the midst of discovering so many things I could not do.

It truly was rewarding to have the means to get myself to various appointments as well as do my own errands. I was able to schedule and attend several appointments to help relieve the stiffness in my neck that I had begun experiencing since waking up from my coma. Meetings with my speech therapist in Amarillo were extremely beneficial. Her expertise focused on helping me in my conversations and relationships with others as well as to remind me of appropriate and inappropriate language to use in social settings. At home, I followed her instructions and practiced daily on the reading drills she assigned me. I was greatly encouraged when my reading speed picked up. It gave me hope that I could someday attain some of the skillsets I had before my accident.

Anxious to find out whether or not I could return to my primary vocation, I began attempting to prepare a tax return. I started with entities Elaine and I had interests in to see if I could still prepare a return. Although I was able to complete them, it took me several hours to finish the basic forms. Whenever I had to research something I didn't know or had to read specific instructions, progress came to a standstill. Based on what I had discovered, it was rather obvious I could not return to practicing as a CPA.

I was extremely dejected for many days as I tried to wrap my mind around my situation. I still had good comprehension of what to do, but the execution, especially if I had to do any research, was lacking. As the reality set in that I could no longer practice as a CPA, I was at a loss as to what my future might look like. It was as if I was standing on a dock watching a ship I had captained for years sail away without seeing any other boat approaching. I was too young to retire but felt too old to learn a new skill and had no idea what might be next. With a heavy heart, Elaine and I decided to sell my CPA practice which I had birthed over thirty years ago and raised to adulthood. While *what* I was to do vocationally was a total mystery, I had complete peace related to *how* our needs were going to be met. God had shown Himself faithful in the past, and I knew He would continue to provide for all of our needs. But it was still a rather sad goodbye.

In the midst of waiting for direction, I continued keeping my appointments with various therapists and working on more openly expressing my emotions. Elaine still believed a therapy dog would be good for *me*, but it finally dawned on her that getting a puppy for me wasn't her real motivation. The truth was *she* wanted to add a new member to our household. The son of a good friend had a Brittney Spaniel being sired to a border collie, and Elaine was anxious to see what the puppies would look like. The first time we went to see them after they were born, we couldn't tell much about them as their eyes were closed, and the only way they could move around was to scrunch. To be honest, I thought they looked more like rats than puppies. They were interesting, but getting one was not a done deal, from my perspective anyway.

Any fence-sitting disappeared on our next visit. The owner shared with us that all the puppies had been birthed in the garage, or so he thought. He found one lone puppy outside, still in its birth sack. This little female survivor stole Elaine's heart, and any remaining indecision was vanquished. We went home and marked our calendar with the date we could pick her up. We also made our first trip to PetSmart. Stepping into an unfamiliar world, I was taken aback at how many products have been created for animals and how many greenbacks people are willing to drop on their pets. I didn't realize it at the time, but we were about to get sucked into the same vortex.

The date we were to bring our puppy home seemed to progress like a month of Sunday's, but the grains of sand finally poured through the hourglass. The day arrived, and we picked up our tiny pet. We had discussed different names as we were waiting but were still undecided until a conversation Elaine had with our daughter. Elaine misheard Rachel's response of "she's so sweet" and thought she said "Sophie." The puppy had a name.

And so, began our foray into puppydom with all its nuances—the whining, the exploring, the playing, and the accidents all wrapped up inside an enormous serving of cuteness. She had only been with us a short time when it became hard to remember life without her. It seemed almost immediate that she became vital to our household.

As the months rolled on, I noticed how many times I thought of God as I watched the relationship between Sophie and Elaine. Sometimes it was seeing Sophie's personality. Other times it was observing how Elaine dealt with her. Occasionally, it had to do with the puppy's actions. But ultimately, I saw visual demonstrations of spiritual truths.

During these months, I started thinking about God's ways and how sometimes they seem a little vague. But it's been enlightening for me to see physical examples of those sometimes elusive spiritual concepts. There's a phrase my pastor uses when he shares an idea that will stretch our understanding. He will say, "Don't hear what I'm *not* saying." I think he uses that phrase to help keep us from wandering down an unintended path. To borrow from my pastor, I would encourage you the same way. "Don't read what I am *not* writing." I am not likening believers to dogs, nor am I making a comparison between Elaine or me to God. Isaiah 46:9 dispels this notion. "I am God, and there is no other; I am God, and there is none like me" (NIV).

As I share spiritual truths I see demonstrated between Elaine and Sophie, I will also be sharing some of my experiences and insights as I recovered from my TBI. I'm hopeful the explanations I share will add some depth. Finally, I want to encourage you to think about your pets, previous or current, as you read these chapters and relate to my reflections. We are all different, as are our pets, and you might go down a different path than I have in noticing your pet's characteristics and habits that remind you of God.

Roughly six months after I returned home from rehab, I wanted to see if I could memorize a whole chapter of the Bible and I selected Romans 12. The first word of verse 1 is "Therefore." A friend of mine from college pastors a church in St. Louis, and I occasionally watch his sermons online. I've heard him say when you see the word "therefore" you need to read the previous verses to find out what it's "there for." Following his advice, I looked at Romans 11:36. "For from Him and through Him and to Him are all things. To Him be the glory forever! Amen" (NIV). What this verse says to me is that He and His ways can be found in a vast array of subjects.

It seems that when people think about God, it's often related to serious problems or major life issues. And while it's prudent to consider Him and His ways when pondering those types of issues, we often fail to see Him in the small or frivolous matters life presents. It's quite easy to ponder God's grandeur when viewing a stunning sunset or standing in front of a majestic mountain. But we can also notice and appreciate his artistic creativity and attention to detail when we look closely at a small ladybug. Not only can He be found in big, awe-inspiring vistas, but He can be located in small, seemingly insignificant details as well. We just have to look for Him there.

During the time it's taken me to write this book, I've started finding God in unusual places, including light-hearted moments. As a young man, I correctly understood God was holy, but I incorrectly perceived Him as stoic and unapproachable due to His holiness. But post-accident, I've begun to embrace the truth that scripture reveals related to God's constant joyful temperament. A portion of Psalms 16:11 states, "In your presence is fullness of joy" (NAS). The take-away is that God is consistently in a good mood and can be found in a plethora of fun places and cheerful things. Like puppies.

CHAPTER TWO
Random Compliance

Our first big goal of puppydom was to teach Sophie to potty outdoors. Granted, there were lots of accidents along the way, but she caught on rather quickly. We were never upset when she used the bathroom indoors as it was a natural function. But we were pleased when the mishaps became fewer and farther between until they were nonexistent.

Potty training a dog has changed during my pet history. When I was a young boy, our family got a female poodle-mix mutt. As part of the training process, my mom rubbed her nose in the presents she deposited inside, spanked her, and put her out back.

We did none of that with Sophie, choosing a kinder, gentler method. Her success with this milder form of training made us wonder what else we could teach our puppy. Our ambitions fell into "the sky is the limit" category.

With lofty goals in mind, we began associating Sophie's next instructions with food rewards. We taught her to sit, stay, shake hands, and play dead. Elaine had to work with Sophie quite a while to teach her to "play dead," but she finally got it, and that trick became my wife's favorite. The progression of the trick looks like this. Elaine points a finger gun at Sophie and says, "bang." She immediately lies down on her side, puts her head on the ground, and stays still until the release command

is given. Then she sits up for her treat. The speed in which she picked up that trick proved she was plenty bright, and we felt it was just a matter of time until Sophie would be an obedient, well-behaved dog.

The first inkling that Sophie was not to be the wonder dog we envisioned occurred after Elaine enrolled her in obedience classes. When they returned from their first session, I asked how our puppy did. The reports were mixed, and Sophie's successes tended to center around food. When she knew she'd get a treat, she followed through with whatever was asked of her. Not so much when she wasn't offered an edible reward.

In addition to Sophie's less-than-honor-student status at obedience class, her other shortcomings manifested themselves at home. She was much more interested in greeting people or other animals and going for walkabouts than following instructions. Although escaping from the backyard or the house could better be described as a run-about.

Her behavior modus operandi was no treat, no compliance. In other words, Sophie does what she wants unless she gets food. Although we enjoy rewarding her, we are much more interested in teaching her to adhere to our instructions. It's not a matter of control or power, but of our greater knowledge and broader perspective. We see what Sophie doesn't.

One of the ways we care for her is to issue commands that help her avoid unpleasant pitfalls. In a lot of ways, obedience is a display of trust—although I highly doubt my puppy will ever understand that connection.

One day, Sophie got out on one of her "run-abouts" and refused to heed our calls to come home. During her romp, she darted in front of a car. While it wasn't a brake-slamming incident, it was heart-slamming because of how oblivious she'd been to the danger of running in front of a car.

In addition to protection, another bonus of her obeying instructions has to do with her behavior. Sophie is a very social animal, and when a new person enters the room, she can't temper her excitement. She jumps on each visitor as if it's a mandate she's obligated to fulfill. It doesn't matter whether it's an adult or child; everyone gets the same jubilant welcome. Although at roughly thirty-five pounds, Sophie's not a big dog, her enthusiastic approach causes people to tense up and brace themselves to avoid getting knocked off balance. It's unpleasant for our visitors and not the way we want to welcome them.

Although Elaine and I want what's best for Sophie, she doesn't seem to care. When a treat is displayed, she goes into her "see what a good dog I am" performance, but without that reward? Her obedience is random at best.

Both her obedience and disregard to commands gives me a small measure of understanding of Jesus's words from John 14:15. "If you love me, you will obey what I command" (NIV). For many years, I believed the main purpose of obeying the Lord was to follow a list of dos and don'ts. I never grasped the relational aspect of obedience. Similar to how rewarding it is to me when Sophie obeys a command without a treat, I believe it must please the Father to observe unwavering obedience with no questions asked.

My agreements with His directives show I believe He has my best interest at heart and is a tangible display of my trust in Him and His ways. Anything less than total acceptance of His instructions reveals a flawed mindset that displays the belief that I know what's better for me than He does.

As I've pondered this, I've come to see the wisdom of some of society's most common adages.

- Actions speak louder than words.
- I'd rather see a sermon than hear one any day.
- Don't talk the talk unless you're willing to walk the walk.

Words can sometimes be trite or meaningless, but actions display concrete evidence that a person is all in. One of my favorite songs released several years ago is "Luv is a Verb" by DC Talk. The lyrics talk about words being easy to say, but hard to put our trust in, and that love is defined by actions. The entire song falls right in line with what I'm attempting to communicate. Although well-known adages and lyrics back up my point, they pale in comparison to the words of Jesus. He states in John 15:13 that, "Greater love has no one than this, that he lay down his life for his friends" (NIV). In clear terms, He lets us know that the action of laying down one's life provides an ironclad proof of love.

God is definitely interested in our words as proven by numerous passages in scripture. But I also believe Jesus shared John 14:15 to show us the importance of taking action regarding His instructions. We nurture our relationship with Him by displaying in a tangible way our wholehearted belief that He has a better approach to life issues than we do. While it's certainly possible to follow the advice of a peer, doing so is on a voluntary basis. When we get to a point in life where we "voluntarily" take action related to His ideas and instructions, our efforts prove in a demonstrable way that we understand His authority. Our efforts prove we're all in. I find it interesting that authority was the second topic He selected to discuss with me after several days of talking about relationship.

By that November, I was beginning to hear God's voice again. Here's what I mean by hearing God's voice. I'm sure some people have actually heard audible words. Not so with me. I realize God is speaking to me when a thought enters my mind that I know wasn't my own. My job is to make sure that thought lines up with scripture since He won't put a thought in my head that contradicts His written word.

While I was at Baylor, and the first few weeks at Pate, my mind rapidly jumped from topic to topic. My initial prayers went something like this: "God, please take care of my kids today. Help Taylor (my oldest son) prepare for his wedding. Taylor! I need a tailor since I've lost so much weight."

Before my accident, I consistently struggled to stay on topic with God, but now my prayers were lost in a world of Attention Deficit Disorder. The best description I can use to describe my thinking process at this point is to compare it to a ping-pong ball. A thought would come to mind, but quickly go bouncing away as it was replaced by something unrelated.

From November onward, the most noticeable difference was my approach to talking with God. Before my accident, I prayed out of a sense of duty, going down a checklist under the misguided belief that rote prayers would start my day off right. Check the box, and my day would be blessed. Don't check the box, and who knows?

As soon as I could hold a thought and stay on topic for more than a sentence or two, I was able to have heartfelt conversations with God on a variety of subjects. As I mentioned earlier, the most common topic God routinely brought up early on was relationship. The other insightful experience of those early conversations with the Father was that they weren't a scheduled appointment to take place every day at a prescribed time.

Today, I seek out the Father without rushing through our conversations to get to the next item on my agenda. It's a practice I've maintained for the past five-plus years. I no longer have a robotic checklist to get through. I have conversations with God when I have plenty of time to discuss topics that need addressing and listen for His responses. It's possible some may not buy into this approach, but for me, the focus has switched from mechanical sessions of trying to earn brownie points to actual two-way conversations with God where all topics are fair game.

Back to hearing God's voice. One morning after I'd been at Pate for nearly a month, a nurse awakened me to give me my medicine and check my vital signs—a daily occurrence I would've preferred to live without. Sometimes I was able to go back to sleep since my schedule didn't kick off for roughly two hours. But that didn't happen this time. I was wide awake, so I decided to talk to God.

It would be a stretch to label this talk as prayer. A more accurate description would be a grumbling gripe session dripping with sarcasm that went something like this:

"Good morning, Lord. It's a great day to be here at Pate. I can't wait for people I barely know to tell me to do hard things I really don't want to do."

I then went down the list of therapists who would be working with me and complained about the tasks they might assign. Even though there were no derogatory thoughts, my healthy dose of cynicism was not hidden.

As I continued to sarcastically rattle on, a thought crossed my mind. *They have that right.*

My immediate response was an eloquent, "Huh?"

The next thought was, *They are your authorities here, and they have your best interest at heart. You should do your best to follow their instructions.*

My mind reeled as I tried to process this new direction. Those thoughts had to be the voice of the Lord. They certainly weren't mine as all I'd done was gripe about having to follow their guidance.

Even though my memory at this point was suspect, and my thinking was still foggy, I did remember God having lots of positive statements about authority in the Bible. The thoughts of that morning were right in line with what I remembered, and nothing I heard was contrary to what I could recall from scripture.

After a bit, I asked God if I needed to apologize to any members of the staff.

It felt like His next response came with a chuckle. *No need to say anything to most of the staff since you've done all of your slandering in your mind.* But He did remind me of two people I *had* actually said things to that I needed to make right.

The first person who came to mind was my physical therapist. A couple of weeks prior, I'd been frustrated about the weird activities she had me doing—activities like balancing on one foot while lifting the other, doing air-squats while standing on a Bosu ball, hopping down a row of squares drawn on the floor on one foot and returning on the other. I said something like, "I've spent a fair amount of time in a gym and know what to do. If you'll just let me design my own workouts, I'm sure I can work up a good sweat and be just fine."

She was an incredibly kind young lady who kept her sweet countenance as she responded, "My job is not to help you get in better shape, Tracy. I'm trying to help improve your balance."

During my time at Pate, I'd often bumped into door frames and veered off sidewalks. But at that time, I didn't realize how challenged my balance was. I viewed myself in my pre-accident form and thought that the exercises given to me were silly and not hard enough. In addition, I wasn't any good at them.

I apologized to her later that afternoon for my arrogant comments. I told her she knew more about activities to improve my balance than I did, and I trusted her. I finished by communicating that I'd give my best efforts to do the movements she assigned. I was okay with knowing that even my best would not necessarily mean I was doing them well.

The second person the Lord brought to mind was my speech therapist. Each morning, the first item on my schedule was to go to her office for a "Vidal Stem" treatment. The best explanation I can come up with to describe this unpleasant procedure is shock therapy for throat muscles. A couple of days before I left Baylor, the staff determined I was silently aspirating when I swallowed. Unbeknownst to me, each swallow mimicked a MMA opponent trying to choke me out. The staff at Baylor forwarded their findings; hence, the weakness of my throat muscles became a high priority once I arrived at Pate.

The Vidal Stem sessions were the only treatments I truly loathed. They felt similar to the kind of shock you sometimes get when you're sorting clothes fresh out of the dryer. Imagine that feeling on your throat, and you get the picture. The only positive was Vidal Stem was scheduled first thing in the morning. That way, the worst therapy of the day was done and not hanging over my head.

My speech therapist scheduled another swallowing test since the prior one had been done at Baylor the previous month. A couple of days after the test, I'd told her, "Thank you for arranging this. But no matter the results, I'm done with Vidal Stem. Whether I pass or fail, I don't want my mornings starting with something so painful."

A few days after that whimpering, woe-is-me rant to her and only a couple of hours since hearing God's direction, I headed into her office for my morning appointment, ready to clear the slate. "I apologize for saying I was done with Vidal Stem. I want you to know I trust your judgment and, regardless of the results of the test I took a couple of days ago, I'm all in as long as you think it's good for me. But having the rest of the week off would be nice since I'm leaving for my son's wedding in a couple of days."

Later that night, I admitted to God I was a bit puzzled over His choice of topics to talk with me about. Out of curiosity rather than anger, I asked, "There are ten thousand things you could have chosen. Why authority?" I got no answer that night, but I was content to wait on God and moved on to thinking about the festivities to be celebrated in a couple of days.

I'd love to tell you my life was different the following days, but the changes were subtle at best. I began working diligently on all assignments given to me and started to hold my therapists in higher esteem. I demonstrated my trust in their judgment by no longer questioning my assignments. And most significant of all, I experienced more contentment and felt like I was making greater progress.

I did get my Vidal Stem vacation, only to start back up after the wedding weekend. But it didn't bother me as much as it had. I also got the freedom to pick what I wanted for roughly ten out of thirty minutes of my physical therapy sessions. But the best news came a month after hearing God's voice. I was notified that I was being dismissed two months ahead of my initial projected release date.

Before my accident, I believed there were three responses to authority. We can question it, accept it, or reject it. But after my experience at Pate, I discovered a fourth—we can embrace it. Authority is such an important issue to God. When people adopt an all-in attitude toward those over them, it honors the Father and gives Him a free hand to accomplish whatever He wants to. And the issues can be ones we've been striving to fix or items not even on our radar.

I'm so thankful He chose to talk to me that day. Otherwise, I never would have seen what He can do when authority is embraced. I'm also appreciative for the experiences with Sophie that have shed some light on the relational aspects of letting someone else lead. And the cherry on top is that it's been so refreshing to take a look at authority from God's perspective - to be reminded that He lays out instructions for us because He truly has our best interest at heart rather than some sort of power play.

After experiencing God's creativity in revealing His perspective related to a difficult subject, I can't wait to find out what ingenious manner He's going to use to teach me something else.

CHAPTER THREE
Either Way, I Get Dessert

Although Sophie has a long way to go before joining the ranks of the obedient, she's at the top of her class when it comes to playing. She sprints to fetch a ball, perfectly judges her jump to catch a Frisbee in midair, and dashes madly after chattering squirrels. She's never caught one, but oh, they're so fun to chase. She also likes to go for walks, although it would be tough to decide whether Sophie or Elaine enjoys them more.

But Sophie's favorite activity by far is chasing a rope bone. When Elaine or I pick up the prized toy, Sophie races to the yard and assumes a full alert posture. Her eyes lock on whoever has the bone, her ears perk up, and she cocks one of her front paws in the air. It doesn't seem to matter if it's a long or a short toss. She goes full throttle across the yard, launching herself to snatch high-arching lobs midair, similar to her Frisbee catching technique.

Since my office is at our home above our detached garage, I often let her nap there and will leave my door open on a nice day. She meanders outside after she wakes up and often returns with the rope bone to drop it with an emphatic thump at my feet. If I don't respond, she picks it up and drops it with more emphasis—as if to say, "Hey stupid, how can I make it any clearer? It's time to play!"

Sophie reacts to the phrase "Where's your bone?" differently than she responds to any other words spoken to her. Elaine will often place both hands on either side of Sophie's face and say, "You're such a pretty dog," or "You're the best dog ever." While I think Sophie likes the affection, she stays put, her expression unchanged. But if Elaine or I even utter the question of utmost importance to Sophie, her eyes raise as she leaps to her feet. She begins to prance around the yard, searching for her rope bone like Indiana Jones on a quest to unearth an ancient treasure. Once she discovers its location, it is game on. One of the things I enjoy the most about Sophie is watching her get so amped when it's playtime.

Her consistent, excited response to those words got me wondering which spiritual phrases have the same effect on me. What initially came to mind was forgiving others, to pray without ceasing, and the Ten Commandments.

All certainly qualify as truths that God has imparted for us to embrace and merit our wholehearted attention. But these are "churchy" ideas that are mostly associated with religious settings. My goal was to identify a phrase I hear in everyday life—common wording that reminds me of God and His goodness. And I have found an awesome catchphrase that meets my criteria.

Since my accident, I try to live by a simple motto that every day is a good day to be happy. The basis for this is found in Psalms 118:24. "This is the day the Lord has made; let us rejoice and be glad in it" (NIV).

Those words are meaningful to me in a couple of ways. First, I'm more mindful post-accident that each day is another day God has allowed me to live. I'm much more aware that every day is a gift from God that isn't to be taken for granted. Second, it's a quick reminder to have a joyful attitude and lighten up. A quick pep talk, if you will, to help take advantage of opportunities to laugh with or bring joy to someone else.

What I've identified as the catchphrase to remind me of Psalms 118:24 is, "Have a good day." This saying, or some variation, is one I hear all the time. When I hear those words, it helps me remember to be happy and smile, while saying something kind or positive to someone else. Life is supposed to be fun. When we only approach God with serious life issues, we limit our relationship and miss a whole side of His character. We need to remember that God wants to interact with us on light-hearted matters as much as significant ones.

Words such as "holy" and "righteous" tend to lead us to think of God as stoic, unemotional, and serious. While holy and righteous are spot-on descriptions, He exists in a perpetual state of joy. Psalms 16:11 reads, "You will make known to me the path of life; In Your presence is fullness of joy; In Your right hand, there are pleasures forever" (NAS).

So, what if you started having conversations with God that weren't centered on the solemn and heavy concerns of life? What if you talked with Him about things you enjoy? What if you asked Him to give you a catchphrase to help alter your daily attitude? The following is a short list of ideas to help you get started:

- Ask God to show you something you find humorous. Proverbs 17:22 tells us, "A cheerful heart is good medicine, but a crushed spirit dries up the bones" (NIV).
- Petition the Father to expose His artistry by revealing something in creation you've never noticed before.
- Ask for insight related to something you are passionate about. For example, if one of your favorite activities is watching football, then request God to show you something unique about the game or draw your attention to a particular player.

The point is to broaden the range of topics you talk with God about on a routine basis. In other words, just hang out with Him. Think about what you do with the people you're closest to and how often you discuss paramount life issues. Usually, your time with good friends is spent watching a movie, playing a round of golf, or sharing a laugh. This type of friend is someone you trust enough to have heartfelt conversations with because you're confident you will receive good counsel. However, your friendship isn't limited to only discussing deep topics.

I've seen the benefit of a catchphrase by watching Sophie's responses. And I've experienced it in my life by identifying one I hear almost every day and have found helpful as an attitude check. While both qualify as solid benefits of using a catchphrase, neither comes close to matching what I experienced about ten weeks into my rehabilitation.

Roughly two months into my recovery, we were notified my stay at Baylor Rehabilitation in Dallas was coming to a close. I had been accepted at Pate Rehabilitation near McKinney. As transportation approached, the packing of all we had brought to Baylor fell on Elaine's shoulders. I had just started walking again and couldn't provide assistance. She gathered all of our personal items; clothing, electronic equipment, and pictures so they could accompany us to Pate.

I specifically mentioned pictures because of the role they played in my recovery. Elaine had read that viewing photographs of family members and favorite vacation spots could help those dealing with brain injuries reconnect to their memories. She had gathered pictures from our various photo albums, and we often enjoyed looking at them during our time at Baylor.

The main reason we chose Pate was that Elaine would be allowed to stay with me throughout my rehabilitation. After our arrival at our new location, she placed the assortment of photos on a couple of small bulletin boards. They hung in our dormitory-style room on a wall close to our bed to help give the room a "homey" touch.

Although I was looking at the same pictures hung on the wall at Pate, it surprised Elaine to hear I didn't remember looking at them at Baylor. It was the same activity of naming the people in the photos and recalling where photos had been taken, but it seemed like something new to me. I remember being able to name all the people and places—except for one blonde girl. Her lighter hair stood out in sharp contrast amidst a sea of dark. My wife, four children, and son-in-law all have dark brown or black hair like I used to—until I started using a new shampoo that somehow changed my hair color to gray.

Elaine shared with me that it brought her a great deal of comfort that I recognized our children, and she was very patient answering my daily question, "Who's the blonde?" Her running answer was, "That's Krista, Taylor's fiancé."

After days of this same conversation about the girl our oldest son was going to make his wife, she decided to alter her answer. Since Krista blends easily with Christmas, she said, "Her name is Krista. She's going to marry Taylor. Think of her as his 'Kristmas' present." Elaine often came up with little tricks to help me remember things, and that one worked like a charm. From that day forward, I could tell you her name although I still couldn't remember meeting her. It was odd that I couldn't remember a thing about her because she'd accompanied us on our last big family vacation in the summer of 2013.

It would be understandable if the photo was of someone I'd met once or twice, but I was drawing a blank on the young lady who spent a week with our family at a vacation rental in the Florida Keys. During the seven-day trip, we had been swimming, kayaking, parasailing, celebrating my son-in-law's birthday and spending lots of time hanging together under one roof. Krista was the only female to accompany the guys on a half-day fishing trip, which was quite memorable.

After an evening of feasting on the fish we'd caught that day, we couldn't decide whether to have dessert at the restaurant that had cooked our fish or try to catch the sunset on the other side of the Keys. Each day we had deliberated over where to partake of Florida's signature dessert, Key lime pie. While everybody weighed in with their opinion, Krista chimed in with "I don't really care because either way, I get dessert!" (We regularly tease Krista about her sweet tooth and definitely trace it back to this trip.)

Despite all the time and memorable moments I had spent

around her prior to my accident, I currently couldn't remember this girl. Taylor and Krista were both so gracious about my post-accident memory issues and planned a trip to come see me a couple of weeks before their wedding. They felt it was important that I not witness my son getting married to a stranger and wanted to start building new memories.

They arrived at Pate late one afternoon, and it was quickly apparent why Taylor loved this girl. It was obvious that she was pretty, but in addition to that, I found her to be warm, talkative, and funny to boot. And the cherry on top was they were great together.

After visiting for a while, we decided to grab a bite to eat before going to see a movie. We voted on Mexican food close to the theatre. After we finished eating, the decision of where to get dessert became the hot topic. We could either get sopapillas at our current restaurant or go to a nearby frozen yogurt shop. We were torn, but Krista spoke up with, "I don't really care because either way, I get dessert."

Left to right: Ryan, Tracy, Elaine, Taylor, Krista, Caleb, Rachel, Joshua

When she said those words, something clicked, and all the memories of our Florida trip replayed in my mind like a movie reel, with images flashing up one after another. When those memories finished flooding my mind, I asked, "You said that exact phrase in Florida, didn't you?" She nodded with a sweet smile on her face. I tried to describe what had just taken place in my head, although I probably did a poor job of communicating exactly what happened. We all shared a pretty cool moment of my memories of her coming back to me.

I had spent so much time looking at those pictures and trying my best to remember Krista, but until I heard the phrase she murmured after eating the fish we'd caught, the memories stayed locked up. I don't have a clue why things happened the way they did, but I'm grateful that I didn't have to attend the wedding of my firstborn son to a girl I barely knew.

"Either way, I get dessert" has become a catchphrase in our family. It crops up at our gatherings when there are multiple goodies to choose from. I think most of our family remembers Krista's inaugural statement at the restaurant in Florida. But those words invoke in me gratefulness toward God for unlocking my memories at the perfect time.

I would encourage you to adopt a catchphrase meaningful to you. It could point to a deeper issue in your life or something a bit more lighthearted. The choice is up to you and God. It's good to be reminded to draw from His endless wisdom or be prompted to delight in His joy that has no limit. But just remember, either way you'll get dessert.

CHAPTER FOUR
Exposed

In case you've failed to grasp it from earlier chapters, Sophie loves to play. While the rope bone is her toy of choice, there doesn't seem to be much of a drop-off in excitement when we mix in other substitutes. We were curious to see how long our puppy would play if given the opportunity. Forty-five minutes is the record so far to faithfully fetch and return the bone, ball or Frisbee. This record likely won't change since my bride doesn't want to try and beat it. Sophie outlasted Elaine, who gave up when there seemed to be no end to Sophie's endurance. As for me, fifteen minutes is about all I'm good for.

When we're done playing, we often let Sophie into the house where she bolts through the back door like the Tasmanian devil. As she rounds the corner, her paws lose traction on the hardwood floor, and her feet stay in the same space despite her effort to keep moving at a blistering pace. It's almost like she's on a treadmill, going nowhere fast.

Sophie's high-octane lifestyle is the primary catalyst for her second favorite activity—napping. Or napping could be her laid-back alter-ego manifesting itself when no one is paying attention to her. But whether it's the need to refuel or the ridiculous notion of her being a relaxed animal, she enjoys sleeping and practices her second favorite hobby often.

Her different sleeping positions make me smile. When she

naps on the couch in my office, she stretches her body along one of the cushions and hangs her head off the edge. When she moves to the cool, pine floor, she adopts the "dead dog" pose on her side, with her four feet straight in front of her and her head on the floor in the "bang" position.

I get a big kick when I see Sophie sleeping on the landing of the staircase that leads to my office above our detached garage. The landing is a little taller than my backyard fence, and when she's asleep in this spot, she rests her head between two pickets on the horizontal wooden base. I often find her out like a light with her snout extended a smidge past the pickets.

I'm a little puzzled as to why her sleeping here brings me so much joy. Is consistently spotting her there when I park in

the driveway a reminder of her faithfulness as she awaits my return? Is it the humor I find in discovering her asleep on her "watchdog" job? Maybe it's how cute she looks with her snout peeking out between the pickets and knowing I will soon have the company of such a wonderful pet. Whether it's a single reason or a combination of all of these, the fact remains that it brightens my day to see her napping there. And it prompts me to remember the pleasure that can be found in the simple things in life, like puppies.

While all of Sophie's positions are amusing, her sleeping posture when next to Elaine is my absolute favorite. Sophie rolls on her back with her rear legs splayed. Her front legs point toward the ceiling, her paws limp, like a queen offering her hand for a subject's kiss. She tilts her head, giving full access to her chin—no doubt because of her love of having her belly, chest, and chin rubbed.

I've never seen a dog stretch out like this. I'm not saying other dogs don't, but none of the previous six dogs I've owned ever have. The most vulnerable parts of Sophie's body—belly, heart, and throat—are totally exposed. She only assumes this position when she's snoozing next to Elaine or me. I've seen her stretched out like this once in my office and I guess it's possible she does it elsewhere. But it seems to me that she adopts a defenseless posture only in the presence of her masters.

Her absolute vulnerability makes me think of the first part of Psalms 46:10. "Be still and know that I am God . . ." (NIV). This verse perfectly illustrates total confidence in the master's presence and is a concrete example of total trust by giving absolute access in a weak and immobile position.

Watching Sophie sleep on her back leaves me with two takeaways. First, Sophie's greatest defense is speed. I've witnessed her easily outrun aggressive dogs we encounter on our walks, but the time required for her to roll over and get to her feet from the prone position takes away her greatest protection skill. Second, I've been captivated by why she chooses to sleep on her back when sleeping close to us. I could be way off base,

but I think it has something to do with feeling safe and protected. Feeling secure with us removes her need to access her greatest defense mechanism, and she expresses her confidence in being safeguarded by assuming a defenseless posture.

I'm somewhat jealous of her ability to let her guard down as she relaxes. For years, I've struggled with letting my guard down around God. I've routinely found it easier to share what I'm worried about than to admit what I'm afraid of. My hesitation to be open before the Father partly rests on being a guy. I've bought into society's erroneous myth that guys aren't supposed to be afraid of anything.

Additionally, I've regularly combined my "macho bravado" with an over-spiritualized understanding related to various scriptures about fear. Two of the more common are 1 John 4:17 which states, "There is no fear in love. But perfect love drives out fear . . ." (NIV) and 2 Timothy 1:7 which says, "For God gave us not a spirit of fearfulness; but of power and love and discipline" (American Standard). Through the years, I've failed to grasp the underlying reality regarding fearfulness. Fear is a real issue—it just doesn't originate from God.

Whether it's due to me being a guy or me playing spiritual games, the result has been that I've rarely been completely forthright or one hundred percent open with God. In the past, I've operated without giving heed to the newsflash that the Father is intimately aware of all the areas in my life, including the ones I'm afraid of.

It seems that at least a portion of the reason God describes David in Acts 13:22 as "a man after my own heart" rests on David's total openness. In various Psalms, David speaks of his fears, weaknesses, and lack of confidence. But he trumps his various worries and shortcomings with unwavering trust in God's capabilities and His goodness. I believe David's complete candidness was part of what endeared him so much to God and stands as an amazing example for us to imitate.

In Sophie terms, I've spent my life sleeping on my side or stomach, but hardly ever on my back. Unlike David, I routinely keep somewhat of a guard up and rarely allow myself to be fully exposed even when I'm diligently pursuing God. I started to write, "even when I'm in His presence," but the reality is I'm always in His presence. Joshua 1:5 declares, ". . . as I was with Moses, so I will be with you; I will never leave you nor forsake you" (NIV).

Up until my time at Pate, being one-hundred percent open before God was a rare occurrence. I remember being terribly homesick during my time in rehab, but I didn't deal with depression or feel down about my situation. Part of the reason could be attributed to my lack of understanding related to the seriousness of my injury. Or it could've been the joy of spending large chunks of time with my wife. But whether it was a shortage of understanding or relishing all the time I now got to spend with my best friend, most days found me with a pleasant countenance and feeling pretty chipper.

The exception to the norm happened the day I woke to the unpleasant realization that my brain would never quite function the way it had before. I remember thinking; *I can't believe I'm now in the disabled category.* I never pictured myself as ever being disabled in any way. It was hard to move forward into that new reality and come to grips with what that meant for me.

Why it hit that day is perplexing as I had numerous earlier hints of my limitations. For example, one of the daily sessions at Pate was "share group." I think the purpose was to help the patients associate with others since those recovering from a TBI often have a tendency to close off and keep to themselves. A common activity during share group was to interact with others by playing games. The leader would pass out cards to various games, and we were to follow the instructions on the card.

Share group quickly became the least favorite part of my six-hour therapy schedule. Shame was the main emotion I felt during share time due to the fact that I couldn't read the cards. I had spent my entire life confident in my mental abilities as I had obtained a college degree, passed the CPA exam, and ran multiple businesses. There was possibly a thimble full of pride in my mindset, but I believed I was smarter than average, and my confidence had been buoyed through the years by accomplishments. To suddenly be unable to read a simple card made me feel stupid. It was humiliating asking for help, and the feeling of being "damaged goods" was birthed during share group.

I had mentioned to God my despondency off and on all day but hadn't had a chance to get His input or allow Him to deal with my feelings. Between turning out the lights and going to sleep, I again shared my discouragement and feelings of discontent. I remember telling Him the extreme difficulty of wrapping my mind around being known and referred to as disabled.

After sharing my anguish, I heard the voice of the Lord say in a clear and concise manner, "Those are man's labels. I will never call you anything other than my son."

A feeling of peace accompanied those words, soothing me as only God could. As I realized in a fresh way how much my Father loved me, the worry and strife I'd been dealing with all day vanished. I spent time thanking Him for reminding me of His care in every aspect of my life and revealing His slant on labels. Labels can be damaging, especially the ones we put on ourselves.

There are a couple of noteworthy points from that remarkable night. When we make ourselves vulnerable, the Father's response is always going to be gentle and caring. His reply will always be kind. Kindness is His nature, and He won't ever act against it.

When you hold nothing back and embrace God's ways, scripture takes on more meaning in your life. I have new insight related to scripture in general, including the first three verses from this well-known passage in Psalms 23. "The LORD is my shepherd, I shall not be in want. He makes me lie down in green pastures, He leads me beside quiet waters, He restores my soul. He guides me in paths of righteousness for His name's sake" (NIV).

The verses that follow these mention some pretty scary places—the valley of the shadow of death and being in the presence of your enemies. But look at the caring and thoughtful promises God makes to help us deal with those hostile circumstances. We need to take hold of the truth that God can certainly bring good out of frightening situations.

When we allow ourselves to be vulnerable and share our fears with Him, we'll rest in a safe and secure place. Our natural inclination isn't to place polar opposites, like fear and safety, in the same context. But He loves this degree of honesty because sharing our deepest concerns shows such a high level of trust. To help encourage us to place our confidence in Him, He makes the place where we come to Him safe and secure.

    I'd like to think opening up about my fears to God will become a routine habit going forward. I want to metaphorically lie on my back with my limbs in the air; all hindrances, obstacles, and defenses pushed aside. When I adopt this position, I can confidently expect to receive the equivalent of a belly, chest, or chin rub.

CHAPTER FIVE
S. O. S.

It would take page after page for me to give you a complete inventory of all the things I love about Sophie. Rather than bore you with a proud-parent list, I'll spare you the many reasons my dog is so special and detail a couple of her best traits. That way, I'll just slip one toe into the "My Pet is The Best" circle instead of jumping in with both feet.

Sophie cracks me up when she fetches her rope bone in the evening. It doesn't seem to matter whether it is day or night—anytime is a good time to play. We have lights attached to the arbor above our deck that provide a slight bit of light as it's getting dark. She'll sprint in the direction she thinks I'm going to launch the bone, often leaping as she makes haste to reach the projected destination. The most entertaining part is the confidence she displays as she makes her blind dash toward the expected landing spot, followed by the change in her demeanor when it dawns on her that she is clueless as to where the bone is, and the resumption of her racing pace once she hears it hit the ground.

I also like watching Sophie when I fill her water bowl. As I hold the hose above her tin, she turns her head sideways and drinks the stream. It looks like she's biting the water, taking chomp after chomp, instead of lapping it up as she does from a bowl. This is my reward for doing backyard chores.

I find Sophie's various facial expressions intriguing as well. Her "game on" look consists of perked up ears with her eyes locked onto Elaine or me. Her "out like a light" facial expression is consistent, but it's her head positions that are different. Her snout can be sticking between pickets, her exposed chin facing the ceiling or her head can be pointing downward as she hangs it off my office couch. And then there is her "I'm innocent" appearance, which she adopts after doing something she knows she not supposed to do; like scarfing up the cat food or stealing socks and stuffed animals. It's almost like she's thinking, *What? You think I did that?*

But my favorite activity by far is to watch and listen to Sophie howl when she hears a siren. One of two interstates that crisscross Amarillo runs a couple of blocks from our home. In addition, one of the busier streets intersecting the highway sits two blocks in a different direction, and ambulances and fire trucks often use this route to reach their destination.

When emergency vehicles head my way, I first pick up the noise while they are a long way off since sirens are loud by design. The siren blare escalates as the vehicles get closer to our neighborhood. Sophie makes no response when the sounds of

the sirens are slight, but she will stop in her tracks as the volume increases, and as the sharp pitches reach their crescendo, she'll stand still, point her head skyward, and howl.

If you've ever seen Snoopy howling in the animated classic, *A Charlie Brown Christmas*, you'll have an idea of Sophie's posture. The tone of her howl is different from those in movies. The howling I've seen in various films is most often emitted from bloodhounds that have a loud, mournful sound. Sophie's tone is higher pitched but isn't shrill or plaintive. Her "a-whoooo" makes a much cheerier sound.

If I'm not outside when I first hear the sirens, I have to secretly move to a window to catch a glimpse of her howling. Sophie won't do it if she sees me or if I go outside when the emergency vehicle gets close. Since she will howl if Elaine or I are already outside with her, I'm guessing it's the sudden discovery of one of her masters close by that alters her focus. And she's never howled inside. She's a somewhat private howler. But every time I catch her in the act, I laugh. It brings me much joy and is always worth the sneaky effort to see.

One day while sitting outside, I heard the sirens, and they were much louder than normal with more than one pitch. There had to be at least two emergency vehicles driving close together, maybe even three. As always, I was enjoying Sophie when it dawned on me that I never hear her howl unless I first hear sirens. As I pondered the fact that sirens always precede howling, I started wondering how many people approach God in a similar way, since ambulance and fire engine sirens don't blare except in response to an emergency.

I've seen fire trucks, and occasionally even ambulances, driving in the city without their lights flashing or sirens blaring. At those times, they assume their role as a part of everyday traffic. But when they receive a call, everything changes. Their lights flash, and their trumpeting sirens proclaim in no uncertain terms that they're in route and speed is of the essence. In other words, their lights and sirens call attention to themselves to allow them to be seen and heard so they can get somewhere in a hurry.

Isn't this how some of us approach God? It seems like some folks don't want to bother Him when there aren't any serious decisions to be made or major life issues to deal with. As long as those people's lives stay calm and in a regular flow, there's no need for them to take up His time with the ordinary. But when life blows up into a crisis, their howling begins.

And rightly so. According to Hebrews 4:16, He graciously provides assistance when called upon. "Let us therefore draw near with confidence to the throne of grace, that we may receive mercy and may find grace to help in time of need" (NASB). He doesn't always choose to solve the dilemma but will provide comfort, direction, or hope according to what He deems appropriate for the need of the moment. And when the problem isn't handled in the concise manner we would like, we need to understand He's working on some aspect of our character.

Many of us don't spend time with God discussing the routine facets of life. Life can be hectic, and some people don't want to add something else to their burgeoning schedules. It's almost a day-to-day practice of "I'll call you if I need you." But when there is an emergency, and their need is prevalent, their prayers can best be described as a howl. "God, I need you. STAT. Mayday! Mayday! Answer my S. O. S. NOW!"

And even more tragic than reaching out to God only in times of crisis, is the blame people put on Him for their adverse situations. God is never the instigator of bad things but certainly possesses the power to keep them from happening. And there is a gigantic difference between the two. He's not the author of disease, the source of accidents, or the reason for failures because it's not His nature. Psalms 119:68 tells us, "You are good, and what you do is good; teach me your decrees" (NIV).

I've never blamed God for my accident. There is no doubt He could have prevented it, but He didn't cause it. I do believe

He intervened that day to keep me alive. It's due to His grace alone that I'm here today to write these words.

I believe the emergency approach is prevalent in today's frantic world. And perhaps the saddest consequence is missing out on interacting with God when life is ordinary. Some areas He may want to grow in us, include patience, planning, and peace. Those words do not describe emergency personnel who must make split-second decisions in hectic situations. Those types of items are generally forfeited in an emergency approach to God as well.

While I am thankful for the quick thinking of the firefighter who discovered I was not breathing when he arrived at my accident, the speed and abrupt decision-making required to handle emergencies is not how I want to live my day-to-day life. Since my accident, it takes me longer to process items I'm unfamiliar with, so I don't make quick decisions well. The reality is there is one of three speeds that best describes me—slow, slower, or slowest.

When I'm talking with God about routine life issues, I find His peace gives me the confidence to know I've thought things through and have given Him an opportunity to speak into my life. An emergency mindset doesn't lend itself to making prudent decisions when asking the Father questions like:

- What life habits do I need to adjust or let go?
- Which people do I need to spend more or less time with?
- How should I plan my finances?

For those who use moments of calamity as the sole reason to talk to God, the chief sacrifice is relationship. Think about your closest friends. Do you only spend time with them when life is rocky, and you need their immediate input? Are the relaxed times spent laughing, doing fun activities, and talking about events of the day simply trivial conversations? I don't think so - I believe the ordinary times build a platform of trust in order to ask for and receive sound counsel in critical situations.

There was one major takeaway from my time at Pate Rehabilitation that showed me there is a better way to do life with God than the emergency approach. I do need to state I never went to Him with a "mayday" type of cry. It's certainly possible that my lack of comprehension related to the extent of my brain injury could have been a contributing factor to my calm approach. But during those weeks, it was almost like I was in kindergarten again as each day consisted of learning new things. Whether it was a lack of understanding, or the excitement of discovering new things, I didn't speak to God with an alarm appeal. And looking back, I'm glad I didn't.

It was roughly two months after my accident before I could stay focused long enough to have a meaningful conversation with God. As I mentioned earlier, what I remember about my first week of spending time with Him is the main topic was relationship. Every time we had a conversation, the importance of relationship both with Him and others, was the chief subject discussed. Whether it was a fifteen-minute chat or a forty-five-minute talk, the theme remained the same.

Before my accident, I tended to fall on the "do for others" side of the coin rather than the "receive from others" category. It was quite humbling to come to grips with being a receiver since I was in no position to be a giver. While we were at Pate, Elaine read me various notes and Facebook messages people sent. Most were from friends, but some were from acquaintances that felt moved to write. She also told me of things friends were doing for us in Amarillo while we were in Mckinney. I was overwhelmed with the outpouring of love and care.

Around this time, it dawned on me that I was alive due to God's protection alone. My gratefulness for His grace blossomed, and it brought me great satisfaction to thank Him for His goodness. I experienced sweet times of talking to Him about His power and the kindness He had displayed toward me.

After several days of these discussions with Him, I shared with Elaine a recap of our conversations. She viewed this as more progress in my recovery and was thrilled I could hold a thought long enough to be able to converse with the Father. I told her, "These past few days, the only topic I talked with God about is relationship. I may not understand this to the full extent, but it seems that relationship ranks pretty high in importance. I think it's more important than jobs, money, education, or activities. It's the only subject we've talked about all week."

A couple of days later, Elaine read me Matthew 22:37-40. "Jesus replied: 'Love the Lord your God with all your heart and with all your soul and with all your mind.' This is the first and greatest commandment. And the second is like it: 'Love your neighbor as yourself.' All the Law and the Prophets hang on these two commandments" (NIV). After finishing, she said, "I think you're right on track. Jesus told us there is nothing higher than relating to Him and other people."

It makes perfect sense to me now why God made relationship His top priority to discuss with me. Although I'd previously read Matthew 22 numerous times, it had never resonated so deeply within me. Before my accident, I would've stated that people were more important than stuff, but it would have come from my head rather than my heart. It would have been a standard, "churchy" answer. The way God led me to focus on relationships during our first few talks allowed me to properly rank people over things in my heart.

In fact, I'll take it a step further by sharing my belief that relationships built during day to day life can offer tremendous aid in emergency situations. When the police showed up at our home to inform Elaine of my accident, she made two calls before following them to the hospital. The first was to our oldest son, Taylor. After sharing with him what had happened, she asked him to contact his siblings along with the rest of our family. More than a quarter-century of living life together gave her confidence that he could and would handle making those calls. Elaine's life experiences with Taylor, from casual settings like playing games to watching him graduate from college and mature into an adult, provided the assurance that he would see her request through. And true to form, Taylor made those difficult calls before he made his way to the hospital.

The second call was to a lifelong friend, Linda, who immediately responded with, "I'm on my way. I'll meet you at the hospital." Years of laughing over lunches, playing dominoes, vacationing, and sharing life had cultivated a deep friendship. That rock-solid relationship was the primary reason Elaine made her the second call—she knew Linda's character from years of doing ordinary life together and that she would drop everything to be by Elaine's side. Linda couldn't help with my medical emergency, but she did bring much comfort during a tough day for Elaine. The support Linda offered in the following days had its origin in their relaxed settings of simple, day-to-day experiences.

Although God certainly has the power to handle any and all situations, He often chooses not to act quickly. But if you've spent time fostering your relationship when life is regular and non-stressful, you'll feel His peace and comfort when emergencies arise. And that will be a tremendous aid while waiting until the crisis is resolved.

Without a doubt, I will continue to take great pleasure in watching Sophie howl. But knowing that's her reaction to hearing emergency vehicles on their way to handle a crisis puts her actions in a new light. And while I am thankful that qualified men and women arrive at an emergency to render aid, I'm also grateful that my relationship with God isn't based on an emergency approach. It brings me a great deal of comfort knowing He's available when a crisis arises but is also available to do regular life with.

CHAPTER SIX
Almost, But Not Quite There

It seems most of my Sophie observations occur during our rope bone sessions—which makes sense because she loves to play so much, and that's the activity we spend the most time doing together. The moment I step outside, she quickly finds her rope bone and brings it to me so the games can begin. I throw, she fetches, and we repeat time and time again.

When Sophie's not in the house, I often see her from a window in our library, standing on the deck looking in. When I catch her intently trying to get a glimpse of us, it reminds me of Gladys Kravitz from the 1960s American sitcom, Bewitched. When we step outside, our vigilant little dog begins a frenzied search for her rope bone. Her immediate hunt for her favorite toy indicates she would like it to be game on.

My favorite place to play fetch with her is from a chair I moved to a prime spot on my deck. It sits between the edge of our house and a large tree. It's a great location with shade provided by the tree and an unhindered throwing radius that allows me to toss long or short, left or right.

I almost always start our play sessions by throwing the rope bone long, setting a glass of tea on a nearby table, and taking a seat. It's extremely relaxing as I love sitting outside in the shade of the tree with a cool, refreshing glass of tea. Sometimes Sophie's excitement is so rampant she forgets she's supposed to return the toy. She reminds me of the *Family Circus* cartoon where the mom gives the son a simple task, and he distractedly makes numerous stops along the way to accomplish the errand.

When Sophie does decide to bring the toy back, it's extremely entertaining to watch her antics on the return trip. Sometimes, she tosses it to herself a couple of times, or she might gallop around some bushes, which isn't the direct route back to me. Occasionally, she plops it in her water bowl while she gets a drink. When she's finally good and ready, she proudly saunters my direction.

She doesn't always make it. At least a-third of the time, maybe even half, she drops the bone on the steps leading to the deck and then runs back into the yard to await the next throw. But the epic problem she can't seem to grasp is that I can't fling the bone if it's not in my possession. And whether it's a sign of laziness or just my stubbornness, I'm not the least bit interested in getting off my chair to reclaim the toy.

One day while playing with Sophie, Elaine came up with a solution. Every time Sophie dropped the rope bone where we couldn't reach it, we stayed put, and Elaine said, "Too far." After a while, Sophie realized if she wanted to play, she had to bring the toy closer.

It's funny to watch her deposit the bone far away from us and leap off the deck. When she reaches the grass, she crouches, perks her ears, and tenses in anticipation. She resembles a hundred-meter sprinter waiting in the blocks for the starter pistol.

But when she hears the "too far" phrase, her posture undergoes a metamorphosis. Her nonchalant ambling toward the bone makes it look like she's thinking, *Seriously? I gotta bring it closer to my lazy owners?* It's a look we see quite often. Sometimes it takes three or four times for her to place the bone within reach of our chairs.

One day, after we'd been playing awhile, I started thinking about Sophie's placement of her rope bone. The initial drop

was often in the vicinity of where it needed to be without actually being there. As I pondered her "close enough" method of returning the bone, it dawned on me that we often take a similar approach regarding instructions God gives us. We follow a portion, sometimes even most, of what He tells us and think we're good to go. We feel like we've accomplished the task and are ready for what's next.

This played out for me the weekend we came home for Taylor and Krista's wedding. We drove to Dallas on Friday to catch a flight to Amarillo scheduled to arrive mid-afternoon, which provided an ample buffer before the rehearsal dinner. I had mentioned to Elaine before our trip home that I wanted to see my bike if we had time. I wasn't able to ride it at this point, but I thought seeing it might bring some substance to a somewhat nebulous event in my mind.

A friend of ours who works as a police officer told Elaine the police department was holding my bike as potential evidence. Elaine called the PD Friday morning and found out they wouldn't release it. The news was disappointing, but I didn't dwell on it as there was something far more important to focus on. It was a fantastic weekend and the days at home were like a small dose of medicine to relieve my homesickness.

Not being able to pick up my bike didn't cross my mind again until Sunday as we got on the plane for our return trip to Dallas. Our Southwest flight was full, and we weren't able to sit together. For the first half of the flight, I thought about the friends and family I got to see at the wedding, the ceremony itself, and what a joyful time these days turned out to be.

After reminiscing a bit, the disappointment of not being able to see my bike returned to my mind. I didn't really understand why it was necessary for the police department to keep it. My accident had taken place more than two months ago, and it seemed there was a minuscule chance of finding the driver. But as I pondered my bike being evidence, my thinking switched to what would happen if the authorities did discover the identity of the driver who struck me. I came to the conclusion that, other than knowing the details of the accident, not much would change in my life. I'd continue my recovery from my traumatic brain injury as a patient at Pate and still be homesick, both for my home and the life I used to have.

I thought about what the ramifications for the person who hit me might be. Would the driver lose his or her license, the ability to obtain insurance, or face criminal charges? I had no knowledge base to draw from, but I had a high degree of certainty there would be negative consequences facing the driver.

It was at this point that I made the decision to forgo pressing charges if the police ever found the driver. The changes to my life would be minor at best, but not being charged might possibly make a big difference in his of her life. I even mentioned to God that not pressing charges equaled me extending clemency. Although I couldn't cite where it was in the bible, I remembered forgiveness being so important that Jesus mentioned the subject in the Lord's prayer. Many months later, I found what I remembered in Matthew 6:12, "Forgive us our debts, as we also have forgiven our debtors" (NIV).

In my youth, I had learned the Lord's Prayer with the word "trespasses" used instead of "debts," so that's the term I focused on. It was obvious that someone had trespassed against me. And since that was the case, I was taking the high road by graciously checking the forgiveness box. In my mind, that issue had been dealt with, and I was ready to move on.

A couple of days later, the Lord brought up the forgiveness issue again. The following thought came across my mind in a gentle manner, "You've forgiven the driver in your head, but not in your heart." While His words were direct, as they always are when He's correcting me, it's comforting to know He never speaks harshly or in an unkind manner.

I asked God, "So how do I go about forgiving the driver in my heart?" Although I asked on several occasions, I got no direct answer. I finally decided I would begin praying for the driver, and God would tell me if He had a different idea.

Awkward is the best way I can describe talking to God about the driver. I didn't know the person's identity or anything about his or her situation. But after stumbling through the first few prayers, it became easier. It was important to me to avoid approaching this like a Pharisee would, so I didn't make it an everyday practice or use legalistic words. I stuck with the clumsiness until my prayers finally became an unsystematic, heartfelt conversation with the Father rather than a quick, daily fly by.

The more I prayed, the more I observed my hidden resentment and bewilderment change into compassion and a genuine desire for good things to happen in his or her life. I no longer felt the slightest bitterness. When I made the declaration to God to bypass pressing charges, there were some negative feelings buried deep within me. They began to rise to the surface and were completely dealt with as my prayers journeyed from awkward to heartfelt. I'm so thankful He pointed out my need to make forgiveness a heart issue and not just a matter of the mind.

I got a slight glimpse into the value of believing something in my heart rather than knowing it in my head. God states in Proverbs 23:6-7, "Do not eat the bread of a selfish man, or desire his delicacies; for as he thinks within himself, so he is. He says to you, 'Eat and drink!' But his heart is not with you" (NASB). These verses describe the true feelings of a stingy man being concealed by his kind words. He knew what was right to say and used those words to override what he felt. In other words, thoughts can be purposely or accidentally errant and obscure the heart to take us in the wrong direction.

God makes it clear that there is a difference between head and heart knowledge. Proverbs 4:23 states, "Above all else, guard your heart, for it is the wellspring of life" (NIV). While what we think is important, He places a higher standard on what we truly take to heart.

Early on after my accident, Elaine was concerned about how I would feel toward the person that hit me once I grasped the seriousness of my injuries. Would I be angry and bitter? Would I blame that person and hold unforgiveness over him or her? As far back as I can remember, I've never assigned blame to the driver, nor harbored unforgiveness. I can't tell you whether forgiving the driver was something God nudged me toward or whether it was something I ignorantly stumbled onto, but I am thankful it's never been an issue I've had to wrestle with.

A major factor in my not holding a grudge centered on the practical rather than the spiritual. I realized pretty early in my recovery that my situation wasn't going to change even if the authorities found the driver. I also decided that my mental state would decline if I held onto anger or bitterness or any of the other negative characteristics of withholding forgiveness. Again, I have no idea whether God steered me this direction or whether the negativity of failing to forgive was lurking somewhere in my mind, but it was a good for me not to go down that dark road.

Jesus tells a parable in Matthew 18 about a servant who was forgiven a tremendous debt, but then went out and shook down some folks that owed him a small amount. Chapter 18 finishes with verse 35, "This is how my heavenly Father will treat each of you unless you forgive your brother from your heart." (NIV). It wasn't until I typed the above verse that the statement I made earlier in this chapter was confirmed. There really is a difference between something originating from a person's heart versus their head.

For those of you who have been sitting on the edge of your seat wondering about my bike, I did get to pick it up in January 2015, after being dismissed from Pate the previous December. As I looked it over, I only found one scratch on the frame and a busted seat. It's crazy that my bike suffered so much less damage than I did. My helmet; however, is a different story. It was so badly mangled, it looked almost disintegrated. My head took a tremendous blow as evidenced by the TBI, but it's pretty clear that I would not have survived had the helmet not done its job.

I appreciate God connecting the dots between Sophie bringing the bone close and my forgiveness experience. Both are examples of right neighborhood, wrong destination. To receive all He has for us and honor His direction, we must take the truth from head to heart. We cut ourselves short by agreeing with part of His instructions to get to the neighborhood, but not all of them to lead us to the specific destination. If we want Him to continue to launch the spiritual rope bone, we have to bring it all the way back to His feet.

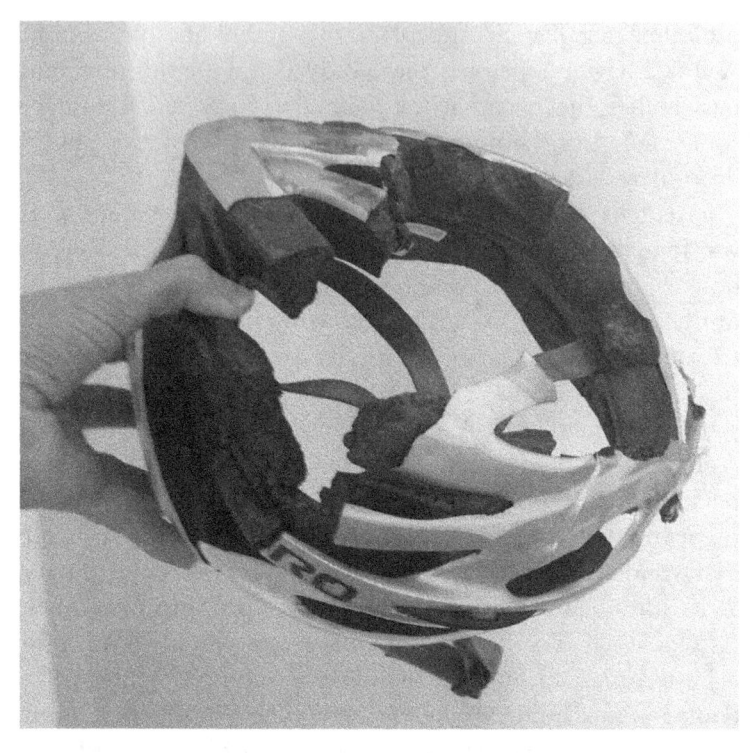

CHAPTER SEVEN
QBKS

I'm not exactly sure why, but I seem to be more reflective these days. My increased introspection could be an aftereffect of my head injury or the fact that I'm approaching the six-decade mark in age. Maybe a combination of both. Either way, I find myself pondering things more deeply than before. Take birthdays, for example. I'm much more aware of, and celebratory of, my own birthday as well as those of my family and friends. Wanting to celebrate the people I love is a subtle benefit of my accident, and one I'm thankful for.

I've spent a lot of time thinking about my accident. Near the end of rehab, Elaine shared with me some of the initial conversations she'd had with my neurologist. In his original prognosis, he gave me less than a 20% chance of survival, and thought if I did survive, I'd probably need 24/7 care for the rest of my life. While I still have ongoing issues, I'm able to participate in triathlons, file my own taxes, drive my own car, travel, cook and thankfully take care of myself on a daily basis. Besides continually thanking God for His grace related to where I am today, I'm also looking forward to what lies ahead. I believe He's allowed me to keep living for something He has for me in the future. This incredibly exciting thought is also slightly daunting.

Thinking about the future reminds me of the past and the way we do things now versus the way we did things when I was in my teens. In middle and high school, I used an encyclopedia or a dictionary to search for information. Rather than directly answer my questions, my awesome mom—a teacher by trade—taught me how to look up what I wanted or needed to know for myself or school assignments. It wasn't that she was unwilling to help, but rather she understood the value of being able to do research on my own.

I also discovered those thick, heavy books served a greater purpose than information. They were the perfect finish line for my hot wheels. Their weight held the track in place, and their thickness stopped the cars cold and functioned as a homemade checkered flag.

The encyclopedia era ran its course and has become a thing of the past. Nowadays, I google whatever I'm curious about. It seems like I blinked twice, well maybe three times, and the way in which we find information changed forever. I guess if I ever nostalgically pull out my hot wheels set, I'm going to have to come up with something else to serve as a checkered flag.

I was curious one day as to why Sophie is always wagging her tail, so I googled, "Why do dogs wag their tails?" Unlike when I used the encyclopedia with the assumption it was correct, I received 419,000 responses to my query that may or may not have been factual. The first four listings were from *Animal Planet, Live Science, American Kennel Club,* and *PetMD*. Although I could have spent hours reading different websites, I decided to limit my quest for the answer to these four. I chose to do so due to my slow reading speed and the sheer volume of data.

The articles stated a wagging tail can mean a dog is happy or friendly but can also indicate more than that. The height dogs hold their tails and the speed it is wagging are critical components of what they are trying to communicate. A low position often portrays fear or agitation, whereas a tail held high indicates interest or anticipation. A very slow wag signals caution and uncertainty, while a faster than normal pace speaks of excitement and eagerness.

Dogs also wag their tails for balance, a detail I'd never thought of but one that makes perfect sense. To follow up on this information, I decided to do my own experiment by walking a few paces without swinging my arms. Walking like this was certainly doable, but it felt awkward, and my rhythm was off, not to mention I felt a bit wobbly. I'm not saying my experiment added anything to the annals of tail wagging, but it did assist me in better understanding the balance issue.

Using insight gained from the articles, I've observed Sophie's tail height and wagging speed change due to her various moods. When I was walking her one day, she was approached by a big, aggressive dog. Not only did she stop wagging her tail, she tucked it between her legs. She also stops wagging her tail when she assumes her "ready to sprint after something" pose. This position consists of her tail held very high, with one leg cocked while being held slightly off the ground. Her eyes are riveted on Elaine or me as she waits in anticipation for the coming toy toss.

While I now realize Sophie's tail wag isn't always a sign of happiness, I do believe that most of the time she's displaying her contentment. In fact, I've observed a couple of nuances about her day-to-day wagging to bolster my belief. When either of us calls Sophie's name as we approach her, her wagging speed picks up dramatically. Her increased cadence is similar to moving a metronome from 100 beats per minute to 160. When we call her name as she's lying on our bed, Sophie slaps her motionless tail on the mattress while continuing to remain in the prone position.

Sophie is consistently waiting for me on the landing leading to my office and when I greet her, her tail wagging tempo picks up. Sophie's increased cadence serves as a good reminder for me to express my feelings of joy and contentment to the Father. I'll often remind myself of Psalms 118:24. "This is the day the LORD has made; let us rejoice and be glad in it" (NIV).

Since I started attributing Sophie's increased tail wagging pace as a sign of contentment, it's prompted me to think about joyfulness. A concordance search assisted me in noticing how often God mentions joy in scripture. Psalms 16:11 reads, "You will make known to me the path of life; in Your presence is fullness of joy; in Your right hand there are pleasures forever" (NAS). Joy also is found in Jude 24, "To him who is able to keep you from falling and to present you before his glorious presence without fault and with great joy" (NIV).

Those verses came to mind first, but "joy" shows up other places as well. A phrase in the middle of Hebrews 12:2 reads, "for the joy set before him" (NIV). Joy is second in the list of nine fruits of the spirit found in Galatians 5:22. I wondered how often scripture refers to joy and similar words, so I searched the NAS concordance on my Bible software. There are 217 references to joy, 113 for rejoice, 30 for happy/happiness, and 5 for cheerful. By contrast, I found 18 references to complain/complaint, 8 for grumble, 9 for bitterness, and 0 for gripe/criticize/whine.

God seems much more interested in talking about the positive than the negative. It could be part of the reason why He tells us in Psalms 100:4 to, "Enter His gates with thanksgiving and His courts with praise" (NAS). It's pretty difficult, if not downright impossible, to truly be thankful and offer praise with a sour attitude.

I grew up thinking of God as cold, stoic, and emotionless. I pictured Him resembling the Lincoln Memorial statue with lots of people and angels beneath Him. He sat on a stone throne, with a stern look on His face, just waiting to zap anyone who didn't measure up.

I never thought for a moment that God took delight in me, so I lived my life with a strict performance mentality. Rather than seeking Him out for a relationship, I did my best to avoid Him and His potential punishments. Before my accident, I don't remember fully grasping the reality that God exists in joy, but I know I experienced His kindness and joy many times during my recovery.

It's possible you may be wondering why this chapter is titled "QBKS." Or maybe you're curious as to how the title and the above paragraphs relate to joy. It's my privilege to connect the dots on those questions by sharing one of my family's favorite sayings with you.

Several years ago, my brother-in-law and niece were on a cycling workout since they were training for a bike race. The wind was blowing harder than usual that day. Those of you who've done any cycling are well aware that a stiff breeze drastically increases the difficulty of a ride.

They were riding close to each other, and Joanna began complaining, saying something like, "I could do without all this wind. It's totally killing our pace."

Bill's immediate comeback was, "Quit bitchin,' keep spinning."

They both began laughing so hard they had to stop pedaling and pull to the side of the road. The phrase stuck, and QBKS was born.

They expanded the slogan by keeping the "QBK" while adopting other "S" words. It was pretty simple to add "swimming" and "striding" to "spinning" to represent the three separate events of a triathlon. The process of adapting it to the triathlon created the unwritten rule of QBKS—you are free to change the "S" word, but the first three words remain fixed.

Joanna is extremely creative, and she took it upon herself to design and print QBKS T-shirts for the races in which our family and close friends participate. Her design shows the four letters printed largely above three separate boxes. The images of a swimmer, biker, and runner are separately depicted in those boxes. These shirts became such prized possessions that it was unanimously decreed by the QBKS board of directors—Joanna, Bill, and me—that for anyone to have the privilege of obtaining that year's shirt, they had to participate in that year's race.

The whole QBKS slogan has provided a lot of fun for our family, but of even greater importance is how often I've used the slogan when I notice myself complaining about something. For example, my normal attire consists of a pair of shorts and a T-shirt. Really dressing up means putting on jeans and a button-down.

Although it's rare, sometimes I have to go someplace that requires a coat and tie. When I find myself starting to gripe about the dress code, I'll say to myself, "Quit Bitchin.' Keep

Stylin'." The other "S" words I routinely substitute into the phrase are "singing" and "smiling." And they seem to help me alter my attitude when I find it going south.

I own several QBKS shirts, but my absolute favorite is the one I earned in the summer of 2015, just a few months after being dismissed from Pate. While I was a patient, I'd been given permission to start running on the campus since the facilities were set on a few acres. Three or four afternoons a week, Elaine and I jogged around the buildings. My wife knows how much I enjoy participating in athletic events and decided it would be a great encouragement to think about doing one. One day she said, "I'll do the first race you choose to do after you're released. Count me in."

She later told me she'd expected a one-mile fun run or maybe even a 5k. At that time, I found it difficult to run at all due to balance issues and was not able to keep anywhere near the pace I used to before my accident. So, she was pretty shocked to hear me say the first event I wanted to do was the Denton Sprint Triathlon. But true to her word, she did the race along

Back Row Left to Right: Bill, Joanna, John (Joshua's Brother)
Front Row Left to Right: Taylor, Elaine, Tracy, Joshua, Ryan

with Taylor, Joanna, Bill, Ryan (our middle son), Joshua (our son-in-law), and John (Joshua's brother). And Joanna, unbeknownst to me, designed a "QBKS—Tracy Hays Edition" T-shirt, which as I mentioned above is my favorite.

So how do all these things fit together? Sophie revving up her tail wagging and the QBKS slogan remind me to take inventory of my attitude on a regular basis. They also help me remember that God exists in joy. He tells us in 1 Peter 1:16, "For it is written: "Be holy, because I am holy" (NIV). I used to think the instruction to be holy was an impossible task, but lately I've come to think of this scripture as a call to imitate Him. Since He is full of joy, I should be as well.

Normally, Elaine and I aren't fans of clothing for dogs, but I might consider a QBKS shirt for Sophie. The "S" would stand for swinging. It's not as if she needs help with tail swinging, but wouldn't that be adorable?

CHAPTER EIGHT
Same Team

What initially launched the idea for this book was watching Elaine's unconditional love for Sophie. I've grown attached as well, but not to the same extent as my wife. Somewhat surprisingly, she still hugs and kisses on our full-grown dog as much as she did when Sophie was little. But I guess that makes sense since Elaine is much more affectionate than she was prior to my accident. In fact, I've watched her affection skyrocket with the addition of grandchildren and Sophie to our lives.

Through the years, I've seen people go totally bonkers over their dogs. Some folks post picture after picture on social media—sometimes more than they post photos of their spouse, children, and grandchildren.

In addition, it seems money is of little importance when it comes to spending on those pets. The cost of some purebreds easily reaches the hundreds and can soar into the thousands. If people had to pay their PetSmart bills in cash, the basket required to hold all those greenbacks could easily double their basketful of supplies. The money flow starts to trickle with acquisition costs but increases to a financial flood through vet bills, organic food, and—of course—only the best toys. If I were to alter Mark Twain's famous quote about dogs, I would change it from, "The more I learn about people, the better I like my dog" to "I'd rather pinch pennies on people so I can spend a boatload on my dog."

The obvious observation is that many people are extremely passionate in expressing love for their dogs. They'll lavish affection on them, display a plethora of photos, beam with pride when someone comments on those photos, and spend money without hesitation to make sure their pets lack nothing. It doesn't surprise me as I've seen this kind of behavior for years. What caught me off guard was watching my wife join the "I'm crazy in love with my dog" ranks.

It would be a close call to determine whether Sophie's overall behavior would tip toward positive or negative. But nothing about our dog seemed to bother my wife. Not Sophie bolting out the door to go on a neighborhood walk-about. Not her ignoring our commands to come back. Not her selective deafness when it came to obedience. Not her pilfering of socks and stuffed animals followed by chewing them up. Not even when Sophie occasionally relieved herself inside our house. Sophie's crimes and shortcomings didn't matter to Elaine—her feelings stayed the same.

The most enlightening aspect of watching Elaine's love for Sophie is that it has served as a firsthand, tangible representation of the Father's love for me. Through the years, I've heard numerous messages on God's unconditional love, but seeing it displayed live and in person has helped me to grasp this reality.

Sophie has fallen short of our standards out of ignorance—when she peed and pooped on our floors as a puppy—and out of willful disobedience—when she steals our clothes and stuffed animals. I'm not sure whether repeatedly jumping on people or bolting out the door falls into the ignorance or willful category, but either way, they're unwanted behaviors.

The amazing thing is that Sophie's actions have no impact on Elaine's feelings. Does my wife want Sophie to quit jumping on people, stealing our socks, and become more obedient? Or course! Does Elaine love our dog no matter what she does or doesn't do? Absolutely! It's refreshing to watch love be so unaffected by performance. Sophie's conduct, even the worst

of the worst, does not take away from her value. Elaine chooses to focus on the joy, not the frustration she receives from our pet.

It's the same with God. He enjoys my company and yours as well. He longs for a close relationship with us and doesn't let our actions get in the way. It doesn't make the slightest difference whether our mistakes are accidental or purposeful, as Psalms 19:12-13 so eloquently describes. "Who can discern his errors? Forgive my hidden faults. Keep your servant also from willful sins; may they not rule over me" (NIV).

The love He feels for us doesn't budge. There isn't a sliding scale related to performance. Or a thermometer where His passion for us soars to a burning one-hundred degrees when we're obedient and plummets to a frigid zero degrees when we're totally clueless of or ignoring His guidance.

God's unconditional love is eternal. But whether we get to spend forever in His presence, loving and being loved by Him, depends on what we do with His gift of Jesus Christ. Choosing to join the ranks of the believer and securing our eternal destination brings us to the inside. Choosing not to, or simply never getting around to a decision, keeps us on the outside. Note that the love God has for every member of humanity, whom He individually created, never changes. The only shift that takes place is God moving a person from the outside to the inside based on a person's choice. It's really that simple.

As newlyweds, my daughter and her husband recognized they weren't always going to agree due to their gender differences, age gap, education, and life experiences. When Rachel and Joshua had differing opinions, one of them would say "same team" to the other. That phrase broke any mounting tension that otherwise had the possibility of turning into a fight.

This "same team" approach is a good way to look at Christianity. There's tremendous value in viewing God as the "coach" of our lives. He's already developed the game plan and calls all the plays. Faith in Him allows us the freedom to remove the performance millstone from around our necks. An earthly coach doesn't kick a player off the team if that player calls the wrong play or makes a mistake. Likewise, God won't kick us off His team when we fall short.

God does have the right to put teammates who aren't accomplishing His objectives on the bench though. Sometimes believers think they have a better way to accomplish something and will call an audible. Other times, they simply don't execute the play. Regardless, it's comforting to know His love for us is not based on results or on what we do or don't achieve. We still get to keep wearing the uniform even when we're sitting on the bench.

As members of God's team, we need to remember His game plan can't be improved upon. Earlier in Psalms 19, verses 7-9 describe God's laws, statutes, precepts, commands, and ordinances as perfect, trustworthy, right, radiant, and sure. The description of those attributes should encourage us to avoid calling any kind of audible and to make the best effort we can to follow His directions.

It's good for us to keep the true purpose of God's instructions at the forefront of our minds, as a reflection of His love. His ways are for our own good and steer us toward the life He wants for us. His directions are not a power play or an ego booster. The Father doesn't need anything from us. Acts 17:24-25 clearly states, "The God who made the world and everything in it is the Lord of heaven and earth and does not live in temples built by hands. And He is not served by human hands, as if He needed anything, because He himself gives all men life and breath and everything else" (NIV).

Although choosing to join His team makes us forever members, we need to keep in mind that doesn't give us license to purposely go against His instructions. The Apostle Paul lays out this concept in Romans 6:1-2. "What shall we say, then? Shall we go on sinning so that grace may increase? By no means! We died to sin; how can we live in it any longer?" (NIV).

Although it's at the opposite end of the spectrum from deviating from the game plan, rigidly striving to perform to an unreachable standard is equally dangerous. In the chapter titled "Random Compliance," I talked about switching my approach to spending time with God from a robotic prayer conducted out of a sense of obligation, to conversations with the Father on a random timeline when I'm not rushing through a checklist. I made a transition from feeling like time with God was something I "had" to do to something I "wanted" to do. This transition is the most recent illustration I've experienced of liberty that comes from veering away from a performance lifestyle. There is such a sense of freedom since I know I can't lose my place on the team even when I fall short.

I'm so thankful for the benefit of watching Elaine demonstrate her love for Sophie without performance being a factor. That's the way love is supposed to be, and I wish I would have figured that out many years ago. I was an extremely performance-driven father when my children were growing up, but now I understand some of the shortcomings of that approach.

I put a tremendous emphasis on the reward system in my parenting. If my kids followed through on an instruction, they earned a reward. If they failed to meet the established criteria, they received no reward and possibly even some sort of punishment. If I could have a parenting do-over, I would attempt to greatly reduce the reward system mentality. And if I were successful in doing so, chances are I would drastically move the needle away from a performance lifestyle to one of unconditional love.

The reality is; however, that I can't have a do-over and must love my children at the stages of life they are in today. No longer do I have the opportunity or responsibility to teach and/or correct on a daily basis. Instead, I believe the best way I can bless my kids is to provide encouragement. To look for real positives that I can point out as opposed to fake compliments that reek of insincerity.

While it's a completely different scenario, I've seen the encouragement approach play out in my writing. I've set up two sub-folders under my *Dog Gone It* main folder. One is titled "In Progress," and the other is "Final." The "In Progress" folder is the location for my initial attempt at a chapter, and where I store the edited documents my editor, Lori, sends me to rework. These documents can go back and forth several times as I work through her suggestions.

My favorite email from her is the one where she tells me to look at her latest suggestions and then put that chapter away. When I've completed analyzing her final edit, I shift its folder location from the "In Progress" sub-folder to "Final." I think of the "Final" sub-folder as the "No Change-Um" folder since the work is complete and there's nothing else to be done. It's truly an amazing feeling when I get that treasured email from Lori to put a particular chapter to rest.

I realize sharing my delight in placing a file in the "No Change-Um" sub-folder might be a trivial description of what the Father does for us when we decide to join His team, but it's a simplified explanation of what takes place. Jesus has completed all the work, and He offers and desires for us to join the ranks. One way His love can be described is "no change-um." He takes great joy in shifting our eternal destination from the "In Progress" sub-folder to the "Final" folder as we make the choice to go from unbeliever to believer.

Sophie will continue to be loved by Elaine no matter whether her behavior improves one iota or not, just as the love of the Father will remain steadfast and constant for me. It's been so good for me to see this tangible demonstration of unconditional love with zero value placed on performance. It's helped make the familiar verses of Ephesians 2:8-9 come alive, "For it is by grace you have been saved, through faith-and this is not from yourselves, it is the gift of God-not by works, so that no one can boast" (NIV).

Performance is a principle of man and isn't a measurement God uses. His passionate love for us won't increase or diminish by our actions, whether they're good or bad. And it's amazingly comforting to realize His love comes with a "No Change-Um" clause and we have the chance to be an eternal member of His "same team."

CHAPTER NINE
Homecoming

This chapter almost didn't make it into the book, but an unexpected event took place that I knew needed to be included in telling Sophie's and my story. I truly believed "Same Team" was going to be the final chapter. I realized that I would have to pen some sort of wrap-up, but I didn't plan on the concluding chapter introducing any new and original content.

Elaine was out of town for the weekend, so I spent Friday night and Saturday morning completing my first pass of "Same Team." I felt a huge sense of relief and accomplishment as I sent an email to my editor. I spent the rest of Saturday afternoon working out and running some errands. I got home as the sun was beginning to set but thought there was just enough daylight left to take Sophie on a walk. I purposely left the side gate open during the walk as it's a little awkward to deal with, and I planned to close it later when we returned.

About fifteen minutes into our usual thirty-minute walk, the skies darkened, and the wind kicked up. About a block from home, it began to rain fairly hard—which is unusual for Amarillo on a couple of fronts. First, it doesn't rain here that often. And second, the rain usually starts as a sprinkle before turning into a modest drizzle or steady rain.

We got fairly drenched during the last couple of minutes, so I took Sophie straight into the house rather than returning her to the backyard. And you guessed it—I forgot to close the gate. Several contributing factors led to my mistake. The sky was much darker than usual. I brought the dog inside instead of putting her outside and, of course, my TBI. The combination of memory lapses and not thinking through the possible consequences of decisions I make are some of the most frustrating aspects of my ongoing recovery.

I didn't sleep well that night, which also rears its post-accident head more often than I wish. Sophie often sleeps at the foot of our bed, and I'm somewhat jealous when I hear her snoring while I'm trying to nod off. That night was no different, and I listened to her snore until roughly 4 am.

Around 7:30 am, I let her out to potty and promptly went back to sleep. I got up around 10:30 and went outside to feed her. When she didn't answer my calls, I glanced around to find her. A sick feeling spread through my gut when I spied our side gate standing open.

Running to the front and loudly calling her name produced no results, so I grabbed my keys and frantically drove around our neighborhood. I asked several people if they had seen a medium-sized, black-and-white dog, but no luck. Feeling sick to my stomach, I went home to figure out my next steps as well as do the thing I was least looking forward to—informing Elaine that Sophie was gone.

In a last-ditch effort, I logged onto the Amarillo Humane Society website where they post pictures of animals that have been found. There were several dogs that resembled Sophie. Each time I viewed one of them, my heart leapt in the hope that she had been located.

It was around 2 pm when I decided to tell Elaine. She was spending the day with our grandson, Lincoln, and I hated to interrupt her day of joy with sadness. I would love to tell you that I thoughtfully opted to text in case Elaine and Lincoln were taking a nap. But if I'm being completely honest, texting

was the easier way to break the news. I dreaded having to tell her that Sophie was gone, and it was my fault—so I chickened out by typing rather than speaking the words.

I was struggling with my emotions at this point in time. For several months, I couldn't shake the feeling that I was damaged goods. It's interesting that I rarely dealt with negative emotional feelings during the time I was at Baylor or Pate. I'm guessing a large part of that was the excitement I felt in learning so many things. Keep in mind that it would be accurate to state I was relearning things that I once took for granted, like walking, swallowing, and reading. And it all seemed new and exciting to me.

My advances in learning and activities began to slow down once I got home. I was, and still am, making progress, but the pace has drastically decreased. As the advances slowed to a crawl and the reality of my diminished capabilities began to sink in, the damaged goods mentality was birthed in conjunction with the realization that I could no longer do the things that were once so easy for me. And letting Sophie escape by failing to remember to close the gate, stoked the damaged goods emotion into a roaring fire.

It's difficult to get an accurate reading of a person's emotional temperature via texts, but Elaine's messages were kind. The focus of our texts centered on the practical things we could do to find our puppy since she didn't want me to feel guiltier than I already did.

About thirty minutes after we sent some texts back and forth, I drove to the pound to look at the strays in person. The majority of the photos on the web had been taken from a short distance away and maybe, just maybe, I had missed her. My hopes were so high; I felt like I was heading to Vegas for a sure win. But alas, after thirty minutes of scoping out cage after cage of lonely looking animals, I gave up and returned home empty-handed.

The rest of the afternoon crept along in slow motion, which was a precursor to the evening moving even slower. It was worse than a snail's pace. When I spoke with Elaine that night, she was extremely gracious and wasn't angry with me, but it did little to ease my guilt. My anguish worsened when she told me she stood in the shower and cried so that no one else would know how upset she was and ruin what had been such a sweet weekend. Rather than throw a pity party, we moved onto the action steps we needed to take, although my hope that we would find Sophie began to diminish.

I continued to monitor the pound website while Elaine reached out to her friend, Becky, who had helped her son find Sophie's sire after he'd been missing for a couple of weeks. Elaine forwarded a picture of Sophie for Becky to post on the

Facebook page designed to assist with lost and found animals.

I didn't sleep well again that night. Although not having Sophie at the foot of my bed was a lonely reminder of her absence, it paled in comparison to the heartache I felt for my bride. Borrowing from Gollum in *The Lord of the Rings*, she often refers to Sophie as "My Precious." I stayed awake a good bit of the night wondering where Elaine's Precious was, wanting so badly to believe she was safe. My mind tends to imagine the worst in situations like this. I pictured her being hit by a car, wounded in a fight, or wandering around hungry and thirsty. But most of my thoughts centered on Elaine's grief if Sophie was indeed gone for good.

As the wee hours of the morning gradually ebbed on, I played all kinds of scenarios in my mind to get myself prepared for a return to life without a dog. Would I be able to help Elaine deal with her grief? Could I ever put the damaged goods mentality to rest and forgive myself? Unanswerable questions rotated through my mind and were as pointless as a dog chasing his or her tail. I finally nodded off just as the sky began to lighten into what I thought would be another long, sad day.

Around 10:30 am, I got an amazing text from Elaine. Becky had worked her pet-finding magic, found Sophie, and was bringing her home around 11:00 am. It's fascinating how a few words can transport you from the bottom of a dark ocean where your sight is severely limited as compared to being on top of Mount Everest, where you can see clearly for miles and miles. I instantly went from exhausted and dejected to ecstatic.

It seemed like half a day for those thirty minutes to pass. As glad as I was to see our friend, my heart soared as I spotted her companion sitting in the car. I put Sophie in the backyard, remembering to close the gate this time, and watched her bolt up the stairs to the landing like it was just another day with nothing of consequence going on.

After seeing Becky off, I hurried to the backyard to pick up Sophie and hugged her way tighter than normal. It made my heart happy to see her, but I couldn't wait to see Elaine's response when she would get to greet our dog.

My energy level drained throughout the day. The relief of Sophie's return couldn't quite offset two evenings of small servings of sleep. Sophie was pooped from her adventures as well and happy to join me for an earlier than normal bedtime. That night, Sophie's snoring was warmly comforting, and I wasn't one bit jealous. As Elaine and I talked over the phone, those snores had a soothing effect on my wife—a vocal validation that her Precious was home.

Once Elaine returned from her trip, things got back to normal. We took Sophie for walks, played fetch with her, and gave her plenty of snacks. It took a couple of days, but what we'd experienced with Sophie really sank in. I couldn't help thinking about the juxtaposition between our despondency over thinking we had lost someone dear compared to our unbridled joy over getting her back.

As I pondered the events of the weekend, I realized I had experienced just a small taste of what God must feel when one of His children is missing. The parable of the prodigal son came to mind as well as the stories of people finding something valuable that had been lost, and God revealed some insights to me.

Jesus tells three parables of people losing valued items in Luke 15 and the conclusion of each story is the joy experienced when they find what was missing. The first parable is found in verses 4 – 7 and describes the owner of a hundred sheep who loses one of them. Luke 15: 6-7 tells us that after searching and finding the lost sheep, the owner gathers his friends and neighbors and says, "Rejoice with me; I have found my lost sheep. I tell you that in the same way there will be more rejoicing in heaven over one sinner who repents than over ninety-nine righteous persons who do not need to repent" (NIV).

Later in the chapter, Jesus shares a similar story describing a woman finding a missing silver coin. Luke 15: 8 – 10 informs us that she also searches and finds her missing coin and shares her joy with her gathered friends and neighbors, "Rejoice with me; I have found my lost coin. In the same way, I tell you, there is rejoicing in the presence of the angels of God over one sinner who repents" (NIV).

The third parable is the well-known story of the prodigal son. It takes 21 verses, from 11 – 32, for Jesus to narrate this story. The ending is comparable to the earlier two parables in that it describes something lost being found. Luke 15:32 reads, "But we had to celebrate and be glad, because this brother of yours was dead and is alive again; he was lost and is found." (NIV)

All these stories perfectly illustrate grace as being a huge component when moving someone or something from the ranks of the lost to the category of the found. As I read about the prodigal son's decision to return home, the passage became more endearing to me. The thought that God didn't make me join His team but waited for me to voluntarily enroll sank in a little deeper. It's a sobering thought to consider that the prodigal son and I both exchanged our poverty for love and abundance. And neither of us did anything to earn an entry ticket into the Father's house; it was simply due to His grace.

I am so appreciative that God let me experience a homecoming celebration with Sophie rather than the pain that would have come from losing her. Even though I was grief-stricken, Elaine's heartache would have wounded me even more. Her temporary anguish made me wonder if some of the sadness experienced by the Father when a person doesn't accept salvation is felt by the other members of the Trinity. Does Jesus experience more grief, knowing how torn up the Holy Spirit and the Father are? I don't claim to be an expert on the Trinity, but I know how much more upset I was over Elaine's feelings than my own. And the intimacy between the three members of the Godhead runs much deeper than the closeness between Elaine and me.

Was it a coincidence that Sophie went missing the day I finished what was formerly going to be my last chapter? Or God's hand? My conclusion is that I simply have no idea. But what I do know is that I got a deeper understanding from this homecoming incident, like so many other events described in the book, when I attempted to view it from the Father's perspective. Sophie's disappearance and return demonstrated such a stark contrast between loss and gain. Celebrating her return gave me a tiny glimpse of what our loving Father feels when a child of His chooses to come home. And there's always a party.

CHAPTER TEN
Full Circle

I want to warmly thank you for reading my first non-financial book. For years I've dreamed of writing on topics other than how to properly handle money. While it was rewarding for Elaine and me to share our knowledge, the technical aspects of finances didn't allow me to scratch my creative itch.

After my accident, I thought those writing dreams were going to evaporate. It didn't seem possible to write when reading was such a struggle. But after rehab, I found writing easier than reading. Although the writing process has its own difficulties, I've found that writing my random thoughts down and placing them into organized chapters is far easier than processing the issues of daily life. Due to the ongoing issues of alexia, I find it incredibly challenging to deal with information that is new and/or unfamiliar.

Elaine described it best when she pointed out writing and speaking are output-oriented, while reading and dealing with my surroundings fall into the input category. I discovered it's so much easier for me to draw from within rather than deal with outside information. And the surprising bonus of this discovery that I wasn't anticipating at all is that writing and speaking fulfill me more than anything I've done before.

I find it interesting that the three main takeaways I got from writing this book were ones introduced early on. I've wholeheartedly embraced them during the time it's taken me to finish this manuscript and would encourage you to give them a try yourself. Based on the successes I've experienced over the past few months, it's my goal to keep engaging in these practices for the rest of my life. Two of the three have come full circle as they were mentioned in chapter one and have made the circuit to find a spot here at the end.

The first is being conscious of looking for God in places other than inside the walls of a church. Romans 11:36 says, "For from Him and through Him and to Him are all things. To Him be the glory forever! Amen" (NIV). I'm thankful to have run across this verse as it became a foundational element that encouraged me to take this project on. It's also a constant reminder to keep looking for the Father in unusual places.

Since I've memorized and become mindful of this scripture, it's enlightening to see where He can be found. I've obviously seen Him while watching Elaine and our puppy, but I'm often caught off guard when I locate Him in unexpected places or circumstances.

The other day I was changing clothes at the gym when the AC/DC song, "Highway to Hell," started blaring over the speakers. When it got to the chorus, the unique thought *we were all on that road and still would be if it wasn't for Jesus* shot across my mind. It would be impossible for me to guess how many times I've heard that song through the years, but I know I've never associated that thought with the chorus before.

I've also found God in other rock and pop music of the 60s, 70s, and 80s in addition to scenes from various movies. Not too long ago, I was doing a jigsaw puzzle and God downloaded a message to me while doing something so simple and ordinary. I truly hope for the opportunity to fill a pulpit someday so I can share this message as it is the perfect illustration of seeing God in the day-to-day.

As I've wrapped my mind around items like secular songs, movies and puzzles, the fact that Jesus can be found in all things has stretched my thinking. My new goal is to become better at discovering Him everywhere.

The second point also showed up in the first chapter; to look for the Father in lighthearted moments instead of limiting Him to the serious ones. Consider how some of your closest relationships were formed. If they're anything like mine, they were fostered by spending time talking, laughing, and joking while doing trivial things together. Those easy times of just hanging out were a major component of building comradery and trust. That trust provides the foundation for leaning on close friends during life's challenging and stressful situations. To say it another way, one of the benefits of building deep friendships during the easy times is that a person can quickly share their heartfelt concerns without describing their goals, hopes, and dreams because those have already been shared.

I believe God wants to relate to us in a similar way—by doing life together. He wants to be more than our Savior, more than a reliable confidante. He longs to be a trusted friend. Lately, I've started talking to Him about dozens of non-critical subjects, like football games, the word scramble in the daily paper, and riding my bike.

A few days after I'd completed a triathlon this past summer, I talked to the Father about my less than stellar performance. I shared with Him that I thought I had trained well and should've had better results. His response was insightful in that He confirmed my conditioning was solid but helped me remember there were factors beyond my control, like weather and equipment malfunctions. Later in that same conversation, my thinking shifted from how I did in the race to the fellowship I enjoyed with my niece and brother-in-law. My focus switched to thankfulness as I thought about the effort Joanna and Bill made to drive to Amarillo so we could all participate in the race together. I appreciate God reminding me that relationship is so much more valuable than performance. Connecting deeply with family and friends consistently trumps the satisfaction that accompanies awards or performing well.

A few days later, I transferred the relationship over accomplishment insight to life in general. We can be extremely well-conditioned for life and running the life race well, only to get caught off guard by conditions beyond our control. Especially ones we don't see coming. As I pondered this and applied it to my life, I thought of the numerous friends, family, colleagues and acquaintances that reached out to Elaine and me after my accident. The love they displayed through their words and actions proved beyond a shadow of a doubt that relationships are far superior to achievements.

The final take-away from penning this book was to try to look at things from God's perspective. Isaiah 55:8-9 informs me that understanding Him is beyond my capabilities. "For my thoughts are not your thoughts, neither are your ways my ways,' declares the LORD. As the heavens are higher than the earth, so are my ways higher than your ways and my thoughts than your thoughts" (NIV). I've found that attempting to see what He sees, even with my limited understanding, has been beneficial as it helps give me a glimpse of the Father's heart. I encourage you to look at life's issues from His point of view. It may not increase your understanding, but it has the possibility of making a heart connection. And, in the grand scheme of things, that's far more valuable than knowledge.

In the Random Compliance chapter, I shared about my first conversations with God after my accident. I will always remember with fondness how God showed me the importance of relationship. It was the main topic of our conversations for the first week. I'm also thankful He keeps reminding me of how crucial it is to live life well.

Remember, the Father isn't hiding. Not from me. Not from you. He wants us to know Him. To find Him. To see things the way He does. But mostly, He wants us to know and believe we are loved.

About the Author

Tracy Hays was raised in Amarillo, TX, and graduated from Amarillo High School in 1978. After attending Amarillo College for two years, he received his accounting degree from Baylor University in 1983. He has spent his adult life working in the financial industry as a Certified Public Accountant and financial advisor. He has co-authored two financial books, *When God We Trust* and *Avoiding the Top Ten Money Mistakes*, as well as four financial workbooks.

Tracy married Elaine Taylor in 1985, and they celebrated their 34th anniversary in May 2019. They have four children; Taylor, Rachel, Ryan and Caleb, a son-in-law, Joshua, a daughter-in-law, Krista, and four grandchildren; Hollyn, Lincoln, Brynn, and Isla. Tracy and Elaine still reside in Amarillo, TX.

Although Tracy has ongoing issues from the Traumatic Brain Injury he suffered after a hit and run accident in 2014, he still enjoys backpacking, participating in triathlons, and staying active. Having survived a near-fatal accident, Tracy understands that tomorrow is not a guarantee and he lives his life loving God, loving those around him and enjoying the moment.

More information about the author, including future books, can be found at:

www.tracyhays.com

Backpacking in Colorado in 2016, two years after my accident

Left to Right: Tracy, Ryan, Caleb, Taylor
Snow skiing with my sons in 2019, four and a half years after my accident

www.ingramcontent.com/pod-product-compliance
Lightning Source LLC
Chambersburg PA
CBHW052028290426
44112CB00014B/2422